CW01095423

GET
YOUR
MIND
RIGHT!

By Adzz the Author

Author:	Adzz the Author
Book cover credit:	Adzz the Author
Instagram:	adzz_the_author
Snapchat:	adzz_official

CONTENTS

INTENTION

I make it my sole intention to write this book in order to help as many people as possible who may be going through suffering in life, otherwise known as trials and tribulations, anguish, anxiety, grief, distress or any other mental health problems. It may be even something that just bothers you, hence I hope you can read this book and it makes you feel better or even helps improve your self-value or life.

"A good word is charity"
– Muhammad (peace be upon him)

[Note: I am no psychologist but a human just like you who has been through some unpredictable events in life, which I had to cope with mentally. I pulled myself through these dark times with fortitude and I share my experience with you in the hope if I can do it, so can you I really hope this book does help you]

DISCLAIMER

This book does not in any way or form advise or influence anyone to commit suicide but rather raise awareness and encourage others there is many ways to escape mental health problems.

Some context of this book is possibly fabricated for the mere understanding of the reader; however most of this book is based on real life experience, which is true and factual. The contents within this book is influenced by the authors own views and experience. No responsibility is taken for any action implicated.

ACKNOWLEDGEMENTS

First and foremost, praise be to god whom without nothing is possible.

For the creation of the book, The Key To Discipline, I want to thank my most dearest and loving my family members, my mum, my dad, all my brothers and amazing sisters especially my countless nephews, nieces and cousins. All who always uplift me in moments of darkness with their brightness no matter what the circumstances.

INTRODUCTION

When I came across various people in life and prison they constantly mention 'positive' and 'negative' vibes, I thought what a complete sense of nonsense and baloney and that was my initial view on this subject. I held a skeptical view about all this 'think positive, be positive' mellifluous. To me it was just a saying that was sweet-sounding and people were tagging along for the free ride of this 'belief' or 'vibe'. However, when I done my research and dug a little deeper I could not deny the solid truth starting at me in the eye, which was there definitely is a golden belief behind this aspect and it is named optimism.

The most troubled of people with their once corrupt minds have welcomed change through the tree of positivity and the many branches that came along with it such as: calmness, composure, fortitude, happiness etc. The evidence for me is in myself because I was a young violent individual with an unsound mind who had no respect for my life, never mind anyone else. My life itself is testimony to the fact that transmuting your thoughts from negative to positive can bring an effective change enhancing the lifestyle of through reforming their mindset.

Growing up I was a nihilist, I didn't care about myself or anyone else and my fundamental beliefs were that If I had lots of money it would make me happy allowing me to live any portrayed lifestyle I want, even if that means obtaining money (i.e. earning happiness) at the cost of other peoples misery. So, I was committing crime after crime receiving prison sentence after prison sentence. In hindsight, looking back at that teenage boy with such crass thoughts and actions he was indeed stupid but no longer existing. Having spent up to nearly a decade behind bars, most of my time was spending studying either myself or the world around me and all I ever did was read or write; for the unsavory source of entertainment was the indoctrination of television, which was mind-numbing. I had to keep my mind alive and healthy because prison is a psychological battle along with an unwanted emotional rollercoaster, which I would not allow to make me any ore stupid than I already was at the young age sitting in prison.

Pondering upon life it evidently has a numerous amounts of duality function, such as heat and cold, happy and sad, good and bad, male and female, day and night, sunshine and rain, joy and pain, mental and physical – there is an endless list. Nothing remains static as we are always constantly on the go in such a fast paced world with rushed thoughts. During this contemplation of life's duality laying down on my prison bed thinking, at this moment is when I stumbled across 'negative' and 'positive' again. What do they actually mean? Writing this book from a prison cell as a convict I have had my fair share of negative moments. Being in prison itself is a negative experience, yet through adopting a positive attitude I have hugged the positive outcomes that come along with it, plus this book is clear and obvious fruition of this golden mental jewel we call 'positivity'.

"In the hectic pace of the world today, there is no time for meditation or deep thought. A prisoner has the time that he can put to good use. I'd put prison second to college as the best place for a man to go if he needs to do some thinking. If his motivated in prison he can change his life" – Malcolm X

I totally relate and understand why he made this bold statement not because prison is the 'best place to be' but rather the time one faces if used productively can bring great benefit forming rectitude and helping others in life. Most prisoners in the system are troublesome who do create their own problems paving a way to a prison cell time and again. As crazy as it sounds, prison was needed for me to 'sharpen myself' because I was not the sharpest tool in the box as they say. In other words, to better myself through self-scrutiny and introspection. Some prisoners are just hell-bent on learning the hard way regardless of how many wise elder men would share their similar experiences with them how their life turned out. Usually, these wise words always fall on deaf ears because of an ignorant young mind. I often say 'young' and that is because it is a profound fact that with age is wisdom. When we are young we think we know it all but reality is we know very little. Age is a time-stamp, something a prisoner has plenty of. Valuable knowledge is not gained through idleness, play and relaxation but through silence, modesty and unique experience observing the world around you.

I do not mean this in an arrogant way at all but having been in over thirteen different prisons, I have met many people from all different walkways of life that I would not necessarily meet in the outside world and it does not allow you to mingle and exchange experience or knowledge, learn new things, understand others, improve your emphatic skills, become shrewd and broaden the horizon of your mind. I often found out that through years of prison-thinking, reflecting and reading plus facing the burden of monotony allowed me to sharpen my mind possessing invaluable knowledge that superseded that of old men because of the time I had to self-study. Hence, through this thing we live called 'life' I indeed have had a unique experience which I passionately infuse in many of my books having felt the pangs of emotion being locked up through my own fault. I do not wish this upon anyone and this is exactly why I share my crazy life I have lived with others in the hope that they can learn or succeed where I once failed. Knowledge is the cure for ignorance, and this is what I intend to share with the world.

For me, I gained knowledge in prison, prison is time, time is thought and thought is change. All these unwanted years spent in a confined prison cell was constructively used on thinking which allowe3d me to invest in myself completely transforming my mentality, demeanor and appearance. I treated a prison cell like a womb to give birth to a new me. I grasped this train of thought labeled famously as 'positivity', which paved the pathway to a better life and intend to share with you how exactly I did it through various chapters I elucidate.

Today is a great time of change and austerity with so many hopeful of the future, yet there are others frightened of the world's state with dark clouds of hopelessness hanging above their head. Life is a package of duality with both sadness plus happiness and we only have one chance in this journey making life itself precious; therefore anything precious must be taken care of.

We should always be in a stage of development as humans using our time as productive as we possibly can, yet for many there is this invisible barrier with numerous psychological, sociological and spiritual crises. Many people carry their future on their shoulders, their problems and troubles with utmost concern, yet struggle to find solutions that are concrete or practical as the valuable mind becomes unsettled or distraught and stressed.

How many are there who allow worries and misconceptions to creep into their mind, making them feel overwhelmed, confused or distressed. There is no complete instruction manual on how to live life for it is unpredictable, even those who are religious attempt to live a so-called 'peaceful' life, yet lose their faith or religious ways or they find it arduous to do so in a world full of grief, temptation and turmoil. Although religions do have a global appeal and mass following providing a systematic way of following guidance and offering a direction even to those with the most troubled minds, yet many do feel burdened with the commandments of religious discipline.

Having to follow set guidelines in nearly every aspect of your life whether it be emotionally, physically, mannerisms, or spiritually is not an easy life-long task to comprehend and act upon. I often say life is a mind-game, and if you truly want to grab life by its horns to take control, then you must first master your mind for true control of life lies in the mind of one's own self.

This books aim at studying, understanding and teaching the human anatomy in specific the psychological factors such as: the mind and thinking, because beings live according to their view or perspective of thoughts whatever they may be. The mind is power and I once read something which I would like to share with you, it was:

"The mind can cause a heaven or hell through for itself just through its mere thoughts'"

The contents and idea of this originated from a conversation with a prisoner serving a life sentence when we were sat in his prison cell discussing optimism and pessimism. Myself serving nearly a decade behind cars understand full well the psychological battles that inevitably one has to face not only in prison but life itself. During this prison conversation different subjects were discussed regarding the element of the mind as well as the faculty of thinking. Nobody has more time to think, read or study than a prisoner and here we were two prisoners having a conversation in essence, which was thinking about thinking resulting in this very book. Like many other authors this book is strongly shaped by my personal experience and what my eyes have witnessed during my life. When confined to a prison cell it can be a negative place, if you allow it to be or it could be your little positive haven. It largely and solely depends on your mind-set.

It was Thursday 7th November 2019 and I remember the television was on in the background whilst we was discussing the various ways of thinking, suddenly my ears caught the attention of Labour Leader at the time Jeremy Corbyn who was running for an election in the coming months, he said: 'how many are there who share their knowledge, yet are impoverished'.

I felt as if he was talking directly at me and at this moment I rushed to grab a pen and paper in order to write down that quote because it touched me. I thought you know what I am going to write this book called 'How To Turn Negativity Into Positivity'. Therefore, the purpose of this book will teach how to try to make the best out of the worse situation.

TOP 5 POSITIVE EMOTIONS

Life is all about understanding through communication and a universal language comprehended by every human is emotion. Many philosophers have stated: 'feeling is the best language'. Sometimes we may experience an event or matter and not be able to explain our emotion, yet we definitely understand how we feel. Therefore, we use this 'feeling' to determine our action or thought. Our mind is always in a state of emotion whether it be negative or positive as we are constantly 'feeling' throughout the day based on our events. Emotion is powerful enough to control your mind because we are creatures of 'feelings'. We feel happy, we feel sad and sometimes we don't even know how to describe how we feel.

'Manifest emotion into motion'

The mind is influenced by what it is fed and if it is neglected than it will accept any thought, feeling or idea. Negative thoughts have a tendency to automatically inject themselves into the mind of anyone, whereas positive thoughts have to be voluntarily injected by the human. You have to filter out the negative from positive and draw upon it to benefit your mental well-being. Otherwise, one may adopt impulsive thoughts, which may possibly bring harm.

It is for this reason; I illuminate the subject of emotion and how to bring it into the motion of the mind. This chapter looks at the top five positive emotions and how you can use these feelings to manifest into useful appropriate action through controlling plus swaying these emotions into ones favour.

<u>Top 5 Positive Emotions</u>
The emotion of FAITH
The emotion of DESIRE
The emotion of ENTHUSIASM
The emotion of LOVE
The emotion of HOPE

<u>The emotion of FAITH</u>
Faith is of two types: religion and confidence. In the context of this book both become pertinent to the well-being of the mind. Faith in religion is very dominant in the world probably now more than ever, with a population globally of approximately seven billion. <u>WHO (World Health Organization) revealed just under half of the planets inhabitants (humans) have adopted a religion of some kind.</u> There are so many different religions in the world from Christianity, Buddhism, Judaism and Islam plus more, yet it is a tricky topic as many become segregated causing division as they do not share the same beliefs. They only follow their way of life and do not welcome any other way of life except if it abides by the religious scriptures they follow causing segregation amongst many and tough stances.

On the other hand, many have become united through the banner of religion as most followers who hold

15

religious belief aim to achieve a peaceful life through a peace of mind adopting a systematic way of life they believe to be revealed by God, otherwise known as 'Divine Law'. Having grown up with my own corrupt mindset strongly shaped by the violently-charged environment I was raised in East London did take a toll on my mental health, but it was religion which was my savior pulling me away from the streets.

I read and read, than researched and researched yet I could not deny the mountain of truth plus morality that the religion Islam promotes. Yes, I am a Muslim. Today the religion has been tarnished by fanatics although the media jump to make it headline news staining people's views on the religion. In short, it is a religion of peace, optimism and positivity encouraging humans to help each other even if it just be simply in any way you could imagine.

Faith is powerful, yet many become skeptic regarding this subject almost behaving their own self that religion is fake, a façade or even some sort of alienated belief. Without getting into too much detail; religion is a particular system of faith, faith is belief and belief is a 'feeling' that something exists or is true. Therefore, the second type of faith is self-belief whereby one is confident in their own set of skills and views on life. As long as either faith is an impetus to your physical, spiritual or mental wellbeing, then it can be something positive and adopted.

The emotion of DESIRE

If desire had another name it would be called 'drive'. The drive for wanting something or wishing for something. Desire is an innate characteristic of every human as we have a lustful capacity within. Every single human has a desire for something or someone and they chase this desire until they achieve it. This gives them a goal in life to accomplish, otherwise known as a purpose-driven life.

Desire is to know what you want. Desire is anything you want it to be, you give desire its meaning. Desire is determination. Desire is a pragmatic plan to achieve. Desire is persistence. Desire is a definite purpose. Desire is not to quit. In the context of this book specifically, desire is a state of mind.

You have to use desire to manipulate your state of mind positively. It is the psychological process of transmuting this emotion of desire into counter-productivity and a constructive way of life, which causes benefit and no harm in order to achieve your aim or purpose in life, it can be small or big.

Desire is just as powerful as faith and the mind itself. The mind has the ability to house any resident it wishes. Simply thought itself backed by a strong desire usually does translate into something physical if not mentally changing one's mentality. Generally speaking, anything that is a state of mind can be cultivated. Desire can be impulsive, but constant desire becomes an obsession, which will eventually consume the mind until it creates a thought to act upon to achieve this desire of yours. Desire is like an escalator that elevates you to your destination (i.e. desired aim). Desire is the plan and aim itself. It is the fuel and location Desire being an form of transport like the escalator gives you the option to get on and off as you wish.

You can use it when you want, how you want and to get what you want. Emotions are temporary swaying from one state to another and you can manipulate them to your advantage. Desire is a strong feeling of yearning.

The emotion of ENTHUSIASM
Enthusiasm is akin to desire, the only difference is you enjoy or have a stronger interest, hence becoming enthusiastic. One finds that when in such a state they do not feel burdened by the toll required as they know the fruition of their efforts will taste sweet once eventually achieved.

Enthusiasm is a fuel that ignites passion into your aims. Desire being a fuel would be named 'unleaded', whereas enthusiasm being a fuel would be named 'super unleaded'. Enthusiasm allows one to convince their mind that they genuinely enjoy their pursued aims in life whatever that may be. This is more of a built-in emotion, which cannot be trained. You cannot learn to become enthusiastic over something, as this would become artificial defying the characteristic or emotion itself. It is something, which comes naturally. You cannot learn joy. You either genuinely enjoy something or not. The same goes for enthusiasm. Enthusiasm is a strong 'feeling' of interest or enjoyment in something or someone.

Enthusiasm is not a learnt trait, rather it is self-installed. 'Feeling' is the cue to know what you are enthusiastic about. You have to experiment with different activities or vocations and some just naturally know their craft they have strong enjoyment they indulge. Enthusiasm is the son of passion. Once a person becomes enthusiastic they know where there passion lies. Like father like son, enthusiasm follows in the footsteps of passion.

The emotion of LOVE
Love in the context of this book is in regards to 'a great liking', rather than the typical love as romance or sexual. When I mention the emotion of 'Love', I mean the highest degree of liking towards something (i.e. I love tennis).

The mind has many emotions, yet all are co-related as we sway from one feeling to another and the body is witness to this as it feels. Emotion is encouraged or discouraged through sense. Love is to gain something favourable. Anything favourable in life is not easy to gain but requires mental and physical effort to equate into its actual physical counterpart.

Love psychologically when obtaining positivity is a consuming obsession of the mind. I know that love is profoundly linked with romance and sexual activity, but pertinent to the contents being discussed I mean 'a great liking'. If love was to be described in other words it would be 'obsession', 'lust', 'desire', 'passion' or even 'enthusiasm'. It is one of the highest format of emotions influential to one's mind frame when intending to grasp a lifestyle or aim in life.

Generally, when someone is romantically in love with someone they usually will do whatever it takes to please that which they love. Similarly, when one truly loves something, then they will do whatever it takes to satisfy they obtain that which they hold love for.

World iconic footballer Cristiano Ronaldo admitted in a television interview that it was his 'love' for the sport of football, which rid of all negative influences such as: indecision, doubt, fear and anything that was too oppose his mind being fixated upon being a professional footballer in his teenage years. Not many know he grew up impoverished in the outskirts of Madeira, Portugal. Not many know that he would often wait at a local burger bar for leftovers at night, yet now he is one of the world's highest paid athletes. A true epitome of a man who had turnt negativity into positivity.

The emotion of HOPE
Hope is a tinge that strengthens the mind. Hope gives one hope. Hope is a inclined feeling that something

20

favourable is likely to happen. Hope is carrots dangled in front of a donkey that it can very much capture and as a means of motivation to keep moving. It is a motivation for humans too as it spurs our thoughts in a positive manner to achieve its aims. Hope can be seen as reserved petrol in a vehicle that allows one to get to their destination. It is used in its most required time of need. When all glimmer of vision was lost, it is hope that comes to the rescue dragging one away from any type of negativity.

There is no replacement for hope. To be hopeful is to be optimistic and being optimistic is to be confident at the slightest of the success or future of something or someone. Hope is not ignition but re-ignition. It sparks up positive feelings lighting up ones mindset allowing one's life to be illuminated, guiding them on the right path towards their destined achievements.

Hope could be described with other words such as: impetus, spur, drive or motivation. Hope is hope itself. When all hope seems to be lost, it is the slightest sunray of hope that reignites hope. Hope can be seen as rechargeable batteries that when low it almost recharges itself. Hope is essential to the well-being of the mind. I met a man serving a life sentence and said *'if it was not for hope I would not be alive' and I am hopeful that good will follow bad and that ease will follow hardship',*

Another prisoner once said, _"even if hope was fake and a lie, that we will not be rescued from despair and difficulty, Would you not like to believe even for a second that you know everything will be alright. That is hope, because even if we accept the argument that hope is false, in essence yes I am tricky my mind to strengthen it and this keeps me positive allowing me to keep moving on in life. Otherwise, the other option is to keep looking back with regret and If I keep looking back then I will trip moving forward. That is why all I have is hope"._

These top five positive emotions can shape the mind:

FAITH:
The belief of a 'FEELING' that something exists or is true

DESIRE:
A strong 'feeling' of yearning

ENTHUSIASM:
The heightened 'FEELING' of interest or enjoyment

LOVE:
When one has the 'FEELING' of a great liking

HOPE:
A 'FEELING' that some good will happen

TOP 5 NEGATIVE EMOTIONS

The need to mention the top five negative emotions holds just as much as importance of discussing the top five positive emotions. Not knowing about something allows one the opportunity to fall into it without being aware, therefore I mentioned these emotional downfalls not for one to familiarize their self but indeed avoid.

It is valuable knowledge and knowledge is like a light, torch or lamp that brightens the mind. For example, a person may be on a journey named 'life' and as they possess this 'light of knowledge' it illuminates their pathway making their travel easy, even to the point where if there was an obstacle or trap; then they would avoid it with ease due to this lamp they hold.

On the other hand, a similar person may be also travelling the same journey 'life', yet due to their lack of knowledge (i.e. light) they become more likely or prone to fall into a doomed pit hole and they struggle possible cannot cope on route to their destination. In fact, due to this darkness they are in such people do not even know what direction they are heading in. This can be compared to life in a way too.

This is nothing but a parable to explain how identifying positivity or negativity is beneficial like a 'light of knowledge'. When one has no knowledge they are left in the darkness of a pit hole almost neglected and cannot be seen, as they themselves cannot identify they are in trouble in order to seek help. Therefore, with these negative emotions it is important to know and the symptoms to avoid them, even so that if you experience them at least you can counter-act them with the correct solution.

I could not emphasise anymore on the importance of knowing the difference between the pair as mental health problems are often caused by our feelings, like that of depression or anxiety. A micro problem becomes macro for the one who does know of such negative emotions because they often feel instantly overwhelmed when facing life's inevitable problems. Hence, the reason I highlight this topic of negative emotions especially the top five, for they are the most common amongst people.

Top 5 Negative Emotions
The emotion of FEAR
The emotion of JEALOUSY
The emotion of HATRED
The emotion of ANGER
The emotion of REVENGE

The emotion of FEAR
Fear is worry, distress and grief all packaged in one. Fear is a mental disease that corrodes the mind. Fear nibbles away at the brains thoughts leaving one psychologically unsettled. Fear is not a physical threat of danger but can be mentally daunting too. In fact, it has even been said that 'mental fear is worse than physical fear' as the mind is kept captive like a prisoner, thereby not allowing one to function.

Positivity is a self-infused fire, which requires no ignition and never dies out once truly grasped. When one understands the benefit it brings they will avoid anything at any cost to remain in a mind-set even if it means being a recluse from those who are negative. Negativity, on the other hand is like a matchstick, which requires ignition to be lighted up. Often you feed one thought onto another before you have compiled a whole heap of problems you may face in the future, which you may not even face. It does not make sense does it really thinking negative.

Fear is negative but can be transformed into a positive, like this acronym below:

"Fear Everything And Run
or
Face Everything And Rise"

You have to pick between the two. Just know that your way of thinking has got you exactly to where you are now in life. Fear is a mental wall becoming a barrier, which must be smashed down by the hammer of courage. Fear is a psychological curse that you spell on yourself and you too are the healer at the same time. Fear must be ridiculed by understanding that it is nothing but a state of mind. If you can talk yourself into fear, then be damn sure that you can talk yourself out of fear and into positivity.

Usually in life when we feel down, depressed or in feat it is because we are experiencing possibly the lowest ebb in our life. Look at me, I was facing a life sentence and this was my lowest point in life but my biggest fear, yet through courage I **F**aced **E**verything **A**nd **R**ose. When things get bad, they will get good. Be sure of that. When you hit rock bottom, the only way is up. Be sure of that. With hardship comes ease just as with life comes death. Be sure of that.

You may not have control of life's unpredictable events but know if there is one thing you definitely have control over it is your mind and this can outwit not only fear but anything that life throws your way but way because mental courage is required otherwise known as fortitude this provides a tower of strength to the mind.

In the religion of Islam, there is a fundamental belief named 'Pre-decree' and it is that everything is written before we were created as humans and that whatever is meant to be will be as god pleases. As a Muslim you just have to try be the best version you can be; this really helped strengthen my mind. It allows me to take the harshest of trials easily.

The emotion of JEALOUSY
Jealousy is the twin of envy. Same meaning, different names. As humans we are judgmental creatures with our wondering eye often becoming covetous. Jealousy can consume and destroy the mind, in the same way fire consumes wood. It is a mental disease that

26

contaminates your thoughts and even poisons the lives of others. It does not allow tranquility to flow in your life as it is venomous to one's mind and nothing good can come from that which is harmful.

Generally, no person is free of jealousy but if one does feel this way they should not pursue it by distracting their mind from jealous thoughts and if it is severe then it becomes an obsession that one should use jealousy in a positive as a means of motivation for their self. Typically, jealousy can be divided into two types:
1) Longing to possess that which belongs to another with resentment
2) Longing to possess that which belongs to another wishing them well

The difference between the two is the keywords resentment and wishing well. When one becomes covetous in a positive manner to gain what they find eye-pleasing without wishing any ill will on the possessor. Whereas, resentment someone becomes jealous in such a negative matter that they almost become fixated to obtain that which they yearn from another person and holds strong feelings of malice towards them wishing they had their possessions etc.

Jealousy in harmony is possible because humans are lustful creatures therefore an attitude of covetousness in peace breeds the positive thoughts of 'if they can do it.. I can do it too'. You should be happy as precedence has been set to follow. Rather, you should train your thought to think harmoniously and totally understand that if someone has already achieved what you desire it is great because you can shadow their steps to gain something similar, if nothing more.

This is one of the finest examples of 'how to turn negativity into positivity', but you and only you have the power to do so to build either destruction or construction. When you weigh up the divided emotions of jealousy it is the sound mind, which picks the beneficial way over negativity. Otherwise, your mind becomes like a merry-go round or rollercoaster recurring in circle on loops which is not as merry as resentment instigates jealousy with resentment. It adds fire to the fitter fueling more fire burning out the faculty of your mind leaving you in a bad state.

The emotion of HATRED
Hatred is a relative of jealousy, if not more vile. Hatred is a strong word and emotion. Whoever holds hatred is indeed a hate extremist. Natural hate is fine, we may hate something but to hate someone is not good but taking it a further step to extremely hate someone is definitely a self-consuming mental poison.

Hatred is venomous and eats away at the mind. It is time-consuming to have intense dislike towards another human. Hatred leads to negativity such as: arguments, feuds and violence. Time is of the essence, so why waste something so beautiful of an ugly trait? By hating someone you make them become supreme to you and give them the residence of supremacy in your mind as you become their psychological slave for they have held your thoughts captive without even knowing. They may not even know they are hated, which is even worse as you are letting them live in your head rent-free!

Forgiveness: the cure for hatred. You mentally develop yourself by adopting such a disposition. You raise your self-worth and character by doing so.

I understand that you may find the person unpleasant for whatever reason as something has happened to trigger this hate but do not let it consume you to becoming acrimonious for this trait will deteriorate your mentality; if not identified and improvised.

The emotion of ANGER
I am way too familiar with this emotion as 'one moment of anger cost me twelve hard years in prison'. Anger is delusional. At the onset of anger one feels hot-headed so much so that a person's intellect is replaced with anger itself and it makes one believe that by harming someone is the appropriate course of action to be taken. In short, it is delusional because it confuses one's decision making skills to think wrong and right and right is wrong. Hence, the saying _'two wrongs don't make it right'_ Greek philosophers such as Aristotle and Plato even the Islamic Prophet Muhammad (peace be upon him) stated: _"anger is insanity"_. If one could extract himself from himself

whilst angry and analyse their thoughts, behaviour plus appearance than they too would agree to this truthful statement. Anger diminishes physical and mental health; just ask any doctor they will highlight the downfalls. It blocks out all pragmatic thinking and embarks upon acts of evil when it reaches extreme.

Anger only exacerbates ones mental condition. If you are to be angry at someone, then be angry at yourself. Be angry at you and allow it to motivate you to do better. Being angry at someone else is double injustice, one on yourself and the other against the person or cause. You are your worst enemy by adopting such negative attitudes or emotions, so you should be angry with yourself and improvise. Conquer yourself by yourself for yourself.

The strong person is not he who can severely harm someone but the strong is he who can control himself whilst angry because anger stems from the devil as historians have stated and the devil is human's worst enemy. Therefore, by controlling one's anger you have defeated your rival through the strength of the mind known as fortitude. One should extract himself from that which causes his anger; otherwise this will only increase fury. If anger had another name it would be called 'self-destruction'.

The emotion of REVENGE
Physical revenge and psychological revenge are both similar, yet miles apart. It can be confusing to comprehend at times, yet nevertheless is a paradox.

The most common revenge known to people is when something harmful is done in return for an injury or wrong. You are upset at something that has already happened and now it has become a consuming obsession within your head to 'return the favour' with violence. This can become a subscription to a never-ending cycle as violence is a vicious cycle, yet it ends and begins with you. It stops when you want it to stop. Every time you throw a punch (a violent act), then a punch is thrown back (a violent act); basically tit-for-tat, therefore it stops when you stop.

Let things be and bury the past with its name. Revenge is similar to anger you want to make what's wrong into right. Anger is the son of revenge, both relatives of destruction. Revenge is also delusional and here is why, because a wise man once said: "How foolish is man! He ruins the present while worrying about the past, but weeps in the future by recalling his past!"

Revenge is rumination and rumination is to go round and round in circles. This leaves one sometimes confused but nevertheless unsettled mentally. By adopting revenge you 'chew the cud' like an animal, hence revenge is animalistic not a trait that humans should adopt. When you behave like an animal, then you may receive consequences that a human cannot bear. Therefore, if you are to seek revenge than the best revenge is revenge on yourself, meaning to improve yourself from your old past.

31

POSITIVITY

In the context of this book, positivity consists of anything that conforms to your purpose, plan or goals in life. It can even be something that enlightens one well-being and lifestyle providing it is moral and ethical. Any circumstance that is hopeful or favourable to you is positive. Any situation that is agreeable to your desired life events is positive, but it is vital to remember the principles involved must be of acceptable morality.

Escaping from negativity can be achieved through adopting positivity and holding tight to it as if it was a rope. Positivity is one of the main ingredients contributing towards a sound mind frame. Through this train of thought; do the fruits of elevation and prosperity truly be attained.

If anyone sees that another has travelled, returning with great profit, then their regret will exceed satisfaction of relaxation. Similarly, if one person adopts positivity and another adopts negativity their differences will be evident. The one who held onto positivity was hopeful and active achieving part of his aims, whereas the one who becomes negative remained idle and indulged in a worthless stale position whether that is physical or mental.

Every wise person confidently knows that greatness and wisdom is not attained through negativity. Therefore, whoever is familiar with the bitter taste of negativity should avoid it. On the other hand, whoever is aware of positivity being palatable will race to seek it. One should know that positivity is achieved through leniency with slow progress; as this constant move allows strengthening of the mind and anyone who knows this will select positivity over negativity.

Life can be bewildering making your mind become a maze, yet it is thinking that is a compass guiding one to positivity. Weigh up the pros and cons of positivity with your thoughts and once you have thought pragmatically, then anyone with a sound mind would coerce and encourage yourself to think positively.

Instilled in every being is the innate ability to seek out right from wrong and wrong from right. Humans are distinctive creatures through the powerful faculty of intellect; therefore we use this to aid us through contemplation, deep thought and pragmatic thinking. Elevation through isolation as isolation leads to this fundamental train of thought known as positivity once understanding the advantages over the disadvantages.

Positivity cannot exist without purpose, as this is the foundation of this sensible thought process (i.e. positivity). One who clenches onto positivity allows their own self to set up new parameters in every corner of their mind as the mind is spacious with no restrictions. No planning permission is required to remove and install a new train of thought. You are the lease owner, landlord and tenant of your mind.

Recognize that you are unique in every essence of your life with your body, mind and soul. Even if the whole world remained positive; know that you being positive is unprecedented because there is no substitute for you. Understand your self-value through your own life experience. You are just as positive as positivity can be. Your life is a product of your accumulated thoughts. Your life is your mind.

Invest in your mind through positivity, meaning train your process of thought to aid you in every aspect of your life. Do not be familiar with negativity as it is an emotional time bomb which sooner or later explodes destroying your mind and life. Every personal should understand these words and follow them.

Understanding positivity is simple. It is thoughts that are harmonious that are agreeable to what you want in life. Do not allow negativity to make you become a victim of circumstance, because our well-being, misery and happiness is determined by our disposition definitely not by our circumstances.

Our disposition can be altered through the many faculties of the mind. Therefore, one should never be radical but if you are to be radical than be radical with your mind through grasping every single iota of positivity you can. Work in your disposition (i.e. mind) and your circumstance will transform.

Consciousness is to be inquisitive. Be eager to monitor your thoughts. Ask yourself questions specifically your mind. Why are you thinking the way you are thinking. Work with your mind through co-operation, rather than allowing negativity to penetrate, working against you. I often say 'the best conversations in life are the ones in your own head' because the mind behaves like a personal advisory therapist, when alone. Humans race to seek that which benefit it, especially the mind but silence is like glucose for this race, in which we strive to find what is best for our mental and physical well-being.

Silence promotes thoughts of clarity allowing one to dig up positive treasures. Use this mental jewel to react to life positively and develop a positive self-image. You are completely in control with the power of thought and decision. Dominate your thought, do not let your thoughts dominate you. Trick your mind into thinking positively.

Do your thinking for yourself. The trouble in life is that generally people hate to think or scrutinize their mind, they confuse their own self by labeling it 'depressing'. Just to sit there and think. I once read:

"what man will do to avoid the labour of thinking"

Thinking is not depressing, but what you think about can be depressing. It is the example of a knife; it can be used as a weapon (something negative) to kill or used to cut a loaf of bread (something positive) to feed others. If you can make yourself believe thinking is negative or depressing, then you can

35

reverse this opinion and make it something positive to serve you in life. Many let others circumstances and their surroundings do the thinking for them. As the saying 'everyone else is doing it'. I have once witnessed someone say "it is raining, it is a rubbish day. I am going to eat a bowl of fruit to cheer me up". If you delve a little deeper you notice that had it not been for the rain, then how would fruits flourish?

The same fruit being eaten in the fruit bowl. You should be glad it's raining due to the benefit it brings. It is all about perspective. Two prison cell mates, one stares out the window and looks at the stars in the sky says 'how beautiful, there is hope', while the other stares out the same window and looks at the ground below saying 'I am ruined and hopeless'. Same window, yet different perception. Just a simple change of thought can transform your state of mind.

You have a mind of your own, use it to generate your own positive thought. Neglect leads to detriment but when you use it leads to strengthening. Therefore, develop and cultivate the faculty of your mind through positive use. Keep your mind secure and safe through thoughts of positivity.

NEGATIVITY

It is equally important to know about negativity just as it is to take heed of positivity, as awareness allows one to prevent their self from falling in the dark pit hole of negativity. You must shine this torch of knowledge on this taboo in order to swerve it. For yourself, it is imperative to remember that negativity is nothing but a thought, yet good news because a thought can be changed.

Generally, negativity has the meaning you give it or in broader terms anything that opposes your plans, purpose or goals in life, sometimes it may not be objective orientated but just purely maintaining a mental state of well-being and anyone or anything that intercepts this pursuit of psychological tranquility can be defined as negative or negativity.

Negative thoughts can be of what you don't want and don't love. It is as simple as that. Some people brainwash their own self by repeatedly telling their self their own sob story and the problem with this is that when you constantly portray a story of being a victim, then this though can, will plus very much does on your mind and shows in your reality. You brainwash yourself to believe that you are a victim of thought. You ingrain this story in your own head, every time you tell yourself that you are poor, unattractive or have a lack of talent, then you are essentially magnetizing these thoughts to reality.

Humans have a tendency to become what they pre-dominantly think about in their subconscious. The philosophy of 'the law of expansion' is real and does exist. The philosophical feature is explained simply:

"What you focus on expands"

Therefore, when you feed negativity with thoughts it breeds more negativity and this is how psychological and ideological questions or mythical stories creep into one's mind leaving the elderly plus young adults confused or baffled at times. You begin to create scenarios in your mind that may or may not even exist, you are as they say taking 'a stab in the dark' or guessing at the unknown.

A negative mindset is empty and accepts anything that is given to it, almost like a dustbin when opened to fill with trash. Life is a journey that can become adventurous but your mind is the biggest mountain you have to climb. Negative thoughts is a mental barricade – if you believe it, you put limits on yourself. Negative within the context of book refers to one state of mind being unfavourable or not hopeful. This is why I emphasise on thinking and thoughts because *life is often not about a change in circumstance, but a change in perspective.* It is about shifting how we view the world and perceive relationships because humans live according to their view, yet by changing this response we can transform our lives dramatically. Train your personal thought process to suit any life orientation you choose.

38

In my teenage years I always used to moan stating 'life is rubbish', until I became a breathing crap magnet to attract exactly that. It was only when I was locked up in prison when I thought about myself and life hard enough to realise that my mental weak thought process strongly shaped my reality. Spending nearly a decade behind prison walls is witness to that, yet it only really took me a few days to analyse my thoughts making me aware of myself and what needed to change.

A psychotherapist once said:
_"the less aware you are of yourself,
the more problems for yourself"_.

Knowledge is powerful and so are you, as you control knowledge. You are your biggest asset and by gaining the knowledge within this book to help shift your perspective or improve your train of thought will allow you to have a "new mind-set". Knowledge can change lives instantly, even if you feel you are in a good space you could recommend this book or share what you have learnt about thoughts.

We have the power to control out thoughts. Many mention the philosophy 'law of attraction', and another word for it is 'freewill' or 'willpower'. We have the power to will what we attract, choose and the only limitations are those we setup in our mind. You do not need permission from anyone else but yourself to occupy your mind and its thoughts. You are more capable than you think. This is a golden quality – the ability to imagine realistic ideas formed into constructive plans to yield what you want from this journey named 'life'.

One must understand that it is natural to feel negative at times because with hardship comes ease, pain with joy. Rain and sunshine when in the same day can form into a beautiful rainbow. My point being, you will be tested in this life but the key is to never give up through a resilient attitude of positivity. Through the acronyms introduced in this book on pages 25, 56, 65, 78 and 85 all of which you will come across and you should use them to block out negative thoughts.

This will allow you to possess the valuable key thoughts that empower you to unlock and control your mind to desirable thoughts manifesting into wonderful feelings to act upon achieving your aims.

Thoughts manifest from what goes on in your mind. It can be defined a 'psychological blueprint'. What I highlight to every person is that the negativity can never be completely removed but can be reduced so its effect is little. We all have felt down at one point in our life and at the root this is negative emotions, which inevitably invite themselves into the faculty of the mind penetrating our thoughts to sway. You will have to combat this time and again with your train of thought through injecting positivity through mind principles revealed within the contents of this book.

40

Recognise that you very much do have the ability to control your own mind. Every idea of negativity originates from our state of mind. If we can change this state by electing our self to become president of our thoughts, thereby choosing only positive policies that encourage one's mental well-being. The mind is subject to direction and control just as nearly as everything else in life is.

We have been blessed with privilege, responsibility and power, therefore we can use this constructively to feed, aid and control our mind as we please. Become the driver of your own journey through creating thought habits.

I grew up in a rough environment of East London surrounded, by knives, drugs and a gun culture, subsequently I became a product of my environment spending years in prison as it has been said *'if you play with fire, you get with burnt'*. I had no control of my thought, I was young with a ripe mind and an impressionable teenager but that along with negative thinking was always going to be a recipe for catastrophe. Therefore, a negative mind frame accepts almost anything that it perceives making one easily influenced.

It is solely down to each individual to influence and control their mind, which eventually allows you to regulate your lifestyle determining your environment. However, if you neglect your lifestyle determining your environment. However, if you neglect your innate ability of this privilege you become susceptible to circumstance often breeding a victim's sob story, when in face you had sole responsibility of choice.

The mind is you and you are your mind. Man thinks dominantly and becomes what he thinks. Thoughts have a tendency not to disappoint but to clothe into an equivalent counterpart of one's reality whether that be monetary, physical or even breeding mental well-being itself. The mind has a mind of its own known and often referred to as the 'subconscious', the thing is not many exert effort to become conscious about their subconscious as they go through life on autopilot programmed or conditioned by thoughts of the past.

A story from the past was once there was a woman and her husband always cooks for her a chicken roast on Sunday but she noticed he would always chop a chicken leg and put it to the side back in the fridge rather than cook it. So, she asked him why he did this practice, to which he replied 'my mother used to do it'. Only the woman rang her mother-in-law to ask about this practice, to which she replied: "the tray was not big enough to fit the whole chicken, so I would cut the excessive to place in the fridge to cook for another day". My point being he was conditioned by thoughts of his past which had of no benefit to him in the future. What we learn as children, or growing up in an environment should never determine or dictate our potential in the future.

"The first and best victory is to conquer self. To be conquered by self is, of all things the most shameful and vile" – Plato (Greek philosopher)

If you ponder upon this citation of the Greek philosopher than I am sure you will derive its wise meaning filled with brevity. How can you not control your own mind? Be sure that if you cannot control your own mind, be sure you will struggle to control nearly everything else in life. How you do anything is almost how you do everything when it comes to life.

The only way to 'self mind-control' lies in the scrutiny of the self by the self. You should observe yourself and the way you carry yourself in life dealing with its matters. Examine your thoughts and what purpose they serve. Psychologists refer to this as 'power thinking' or 'intelligent self-analysis'.

Understand negativity is worthless and trivial, therefore keep a far distance from it by taking care of your personal mind through adopting sole thoughts of positivity and embrace them regularly by habit.

TURNING NEGATIVITY INTO POSITIVITY

Identification. Awareness. Scrutiny. Understanding. Examination. All the words correlate to 'change' and 'rehabilitation'. Transmutation is at the core of altering one's thoughts from negative to positive.

A perfect code of life is arduous as there are so many diverse human concerns that need to be addressed in different stages of life. There are many calamities or dilemmas faced by both the young and elderly as they face grief, distress, worry allowing misconceptions to crawl into their mind, leaving one unsettled mentally and as a result drenched in negativity. However, the aim of this book is to help you grasp easy psychological techniques to escape negativity by strengthening one's ideological state.

Examination is imperative as it allows introspection of your thoughts. You should know that when a doctor treats a disease, they consider the patients attributes such as: age, health, genetics etc. Once this has been inspected the doctor than prescribes medicine accordingly. Therefore, a similar approach should be taken to your thoughts as the mind becomes an advisory doctor.

Generally, our cognition has a paramount effect on our thoughts and this is undeniable. Your thoughts are either positive or negative and you must learn to identify when plus how this can benefit you when it is positive, but even better transform a negative into a positive. It is when people often say: 'make the best

44

out of a worse situation'. Positivity is a beautiful trait and it is a serving quality to the mind in the same sense of what carbon is to steel. Positivity is strength, negativity is weak, and weak motivation stems into weak results, in the same way a weak fire produces weak results. Scrutinize your thoughts and this is the unexpected or expected turn to positivity. You can indulge in life viewing things to be an obstacle or opportunity, one being negative and the other being positive.

> *"Obstacles are those frightful things you see when you take your eyes off your goals"* – Henry Ford

Learn to polish your mind through thinking positively and focusing on your goals whatever they may be. See good in everything and the good in every bad situation you may find yourself in. If you have been through some negative situations and your past is tough but you are still trying to be positive that shows a real resilience about your character.

I have spent nearly a decade behind prison walls and indeed the consequences of prison seem never-ending with bad news after bad news whilst you are locked up, isolated plus cannot offer any assistance to your loved ones in terms of being there physically, as well as being there psychologically castrated from those who you closely associate with. Prison holds the worst of society under one roof, all to co-exist amongst each other in a violently-charged atmosphere. However, with a simple 'change of thought' I chose

45

prison to be a university rather than a dumping ground, meaning I used my time constructively to learn, read, write and even take it further by writing several books including this one. I saw the good in bad, made the best out of a worst situation and turnt something negative into a positive through my train of thought, which I will shape with you and this is exactly what qualifies me to elucidate this subject as an author.

A glowing example of negative to positive is pain to strength. I once read: *'the pain you feel today is the strength you feel tomorrow'*, this can apply to the principles of resilience. No matter how many times you fall, you still get back up.

Also, anyone who works out in the gym understands that your body must endure pain before the process of your muscles strengthens. This goes for any muscle or organ even the mind included. Through hardship you become familiar with ease. A student may feel pangs of burdens such as: hard work and monotony, yet later blossoms into an expert in their studied field as scholars. It is a tough process with darkness as the beginning but they shine in the end.

It comes down to your disposition over circumstance or as many famously say 'mind over matter'. Positivity exists from ancient times if not the beginning and is highlighted by teachers, poets, prophets and philosophers. Everything beautiful originates from a positive force. You have control over the power of positivity, which resides in your mind but you just need to tap into it. You can choose to use it or lose it. Choice is extremely powerful.

Experience is cognition because of the innate ability to senses we possess. In fact, every iota of a moment when you experience something you like that is positive and good but when it is something you do not like it could be negative. However, this depends purely on disposition and circumstance. For example, me coming to prison was a negative in the eyes of many but a positive to me because it reformed me and allowed me to sharpen my mindset plus would I have ever had the time to reflect and rectify my ways if I had never come back prison. What I mean is sometimes you may find a thing is bad for you but can turn out to be food for you, whereas sometimes also you may think something is good for you but indeed it is bad, yet this is determined by your sense of judgment only.

Controlling your senses (i.e. cognition) is just as important as controlling your thoughts. It solely is 'mind over matter', no matter who you are, no matter the circumstance,, no matter what you may be facing – you can trick your mind and coerce it into positivity. I am not asking you to lie yourself, but be realistic within the scope of your life and genuinely seek the good purposely every time you may find yourself in a bad situation, remember that things potentially could have been worse with different outcomes.

Imagination is determination. Imagine what you want and let it determine you. Many imagine the worst and as a result live in fear, yet if you reverse this thought process, then you can also imagine the best and as a result live in hope instead. Choice is yours. Thoughts only have the value you give it. In short, you must imagine the opposite of a negative condition you may find yourself in, in order to achieve positivity. Think positive, do positive, and feel positive.

Feed your thoughts positivity and starve it from negativity. You become what you dominantly think as thoughts have a tendency of manifesting into reality. Your mind is a tool or weapon no different from a knife it can benefit or harm you. You can use a knife to harm someone or cut a loaf of bread to feed yourself and others. Your thoughts drive you like a car with its engine and steering wheel that you must control! You are the driver of your mind! Tame your hostile thoughts (i.e. negativity) through positivity! Awareness through observation allows control of thought. Analyse your thoughts and what purpose they serve. Concentrate on your thoughts. Pay attention to your thoughts. If you want to know yourself, know your thoughts. You give your thoughts the meaning you want.

William Shakespeare once said: "nothing is either good or bad, but thinking makes it so" (1564-1616)

Thought is a magnificent tool that is invisible making it untouchable. You are your thoughts or you choose

48

your thoughts to become you. Negativity in precedent ancient times has been strongly linked with anger, badness, and evil plus at times even been associated with "the devil" (just as I mentioned on page 30). This was because of those who had fallen into depression in the 'depression era' and as a result committed suicide. Hence, dubbing 'negativity' or 'negative thoughts' as the whispers of the devil.

Positivity is a light, which allows you to shine in life. Positivity is a mental art, which transmutes defeat into opportunity, pain into strength, and hardship into ease and destruction into construction. It is important to note like the body, the mind requires life-long maintenance, caring and nourishment. It is not something to be left alone to wander with its thoughts as it is very much essentially in need of constant analysis from time to time. Take out time weekly or monthly to scrutinize yourself or thoughts.

Do I think negative all the time?
Am I a pessimist or optimist?

These types of questions are important as it gives you more understanding about yourself. Observing your thoughts is the primary way to channel and inject positivity, thereby ejecting negativity. Your thoughts are your mind and your mind is your thoughts. The minds thoughts can be referred to as the 'sub-conscious'.

Manipulate your subconscious and your conscious follows. Voluntarily inject positivity through encouragement and discourage negativity. Humans whether they like it or not are selfish creatures. If it came to life and death, yet they had to pick their self to save or someone else, than the self always comes first. Humans race to seek that which benefits their own self. Therefore, naturally the mind will adopt positivity once it understands the threats of negativity. Dominate your subconscious with positivity and negativity will be eliminated.

IMPORTANT NOTE:
The main principle behind turning negativity into positivity is as simple as this:

o   Look on the bright side
o   Remember things could be the worse
o   See the good in every bad (make a list if need be)
o   Time is a healer, things will get better

Make a journal of your thoughts and scrutinise it
What I am encouraging in this chapter is for you to train your mind for there is no bigger education than this concept. Intelligent people understand that sharpening or developing your mind is the greatest asset in life, this can be known as 'investing in yourself'. Human beings live according to their views and thoughts, which is strongly determined by their state of mind. Muscles develop through use and the same principle applies to the mind.

Educated people are unanimously familiar that one's mindset is true capital, as your mind travels with you everywhere you go. Use the faculty of your brain (i.e. mind) to select only positive choices, which determine your lifestyle and circumstance ultimately. Affluent men and women are not fixated with money, but obsessed with their mindset being rich; they have associated being poor with negativity and being wealthy with positivity.

After all, you cannot help the poor being one of them. They have convinced their inner self (i.e. subconscious thoughts) that being poor is negative and this does not resonate in their mind as they only strive to seek the actions or mindset of a rich person. They know full well money is freedom allowing them the opportunity to be capitalists helping society and those less fortunate, ultimately contributing towards the lives of others positively.

Positive thoughts are like an exalted plane, which lifts one's thinking above ordinary thought to aid one towards their coveted purpose in life. True freedom lies in your mind and process of thought.

Nelson Mandela understood this concept full well when he served over twenty-five years in prison. When asked how he coped he said: *"my physical liberty may be taken but the freedom of my mind certainly not".* This was a man who stood up against racism and egregious behaviour for an egalitarian society through his positive mindset, despite enduring the hardships of prison. Not only did he manifest equality but become president of his country! There is no predicting what positivity brings!

Negativity works within our subconscious and positivity within our conscious. Negativity self-injects, whereas positivity needs to be injected. Awareness, introspection, examination and consciousness are all types of psychological needles with positivity ready for injection. So many thoughts drift in and out of the mind but don't really amount to anything because maybe we don't pay enough attention with our conscious.

Looking at the faculty of the mind such as the subconscious, it does self-function whether you exert effort or not almost like auto-pilot mode. It organically brings about thoughts associated with negativity including fear (like I mentioned on page 14 with the top five negative emotions).

What is important is how we react to these thoughts because they will never be able to be completely expunged. Even the wealthiest of business people know that there is a fear of risk going into business, but they shift their attention from obstacles into opportunity with calculated decision-making, once research is completed appropriately, hence turning fear itself into an opportunity – a negative into a positive.

All I am asking is just scrutinize your thoughts from time to time and try pick up on little hunches of when you are thinking negatively. Make a journal of your thoughts and at the end of the week go through them.

This will allow you to influence your subconscious thoughts by making it susceptible to your coveted goals through the positive emotion of 'desire'. Your feelings when mixed with your thoughts is an undefeatable combination to positivity.
Sound reason completely understands that emotion stirred with thoughts does manifest into your chosen desires. This is known as 'emotionalised thoughts', which strongly does effect the sub-conscious mind, in essence allowing you to control your minds through essentially transmitting negative into positive.

The subconscious mind is the driver of the mind. Master your mind through dominating the subconscious thoughts. Your inner mind (i.e. subconscious) is like a machine that does turn off; it never remains idle and is always working. If you do not feed it thoughts of positivity, it will act on impulse on any negative channel of thought as a result of neglect. Hence, a negative mind accepts anything (i.e. any suggestion or thought) that is given to it. An impulsive thought is indeed 'cold' with no emotion freezing the subconscious with negativity allowing positivity to slip away.

The mind especially the subconscious is intangible and completely willing to be in your domain but you must control it through self-suggestion.

Self-suggestion is to acknowledge your state of mind using your emotions as the measurement.

How do negative thoughts truly make you feel in comparison to positivity?

Your mind is subjective to control through self-instruction or even self-analysis. This allows one to disclose their strengths and weaknesses that you may not necessarily like to acknowledge. Rise above mediocrity through self-examination. In a fast paced world, which is short-lived people are rushing to seek a living with hardly time set aside for introspection. Leading to the famous saying:

"Do not work so hard earning a livelihood, that you forget to make a living"

The privilege of thinking often goes underestimated. You may control your mind through a simple change of thought. You have the ability of construction and destruction of your mind. You may not be able to control life's events when they unfold, but be sure to control your own mind at least. Exercise this innate right of yours to enhance your mental well-being. Banish any negative thoughts and hug any positivity.

Mind-control (otherwise referred to as controlling your mind can be achieved through self-indoctrination. Convince yourself to believe your desired thoughts. If you can perceive, you can achieve. Do not compromise with negativity because just one negative thought is effacious enough to corrupt the mind, in the same way one drop of ink in clear water alters its aesthetic. It is noteworthy that for you to achieve your aims and be successful you must gain control over your own mind. There is no other way to positivity.

Silence is at the core of allowing one to inspect their thoughts and gain control over every inch or corner of your mind! Silence is a stimulant for thinking, thinking allows self-analysis, self-analysis promotes positivity, positivity leads to purpose and purpose leads to mind-control. Knowing what you want in life. Here is a great autodidact technique I use to allow me to transform my thoughts from negative to positive because I do when negativity creeps into my mind is simply STOP!

Silently Think Of Positivity
STOP is like a brake that is pushed before a calamity of a car crash appears or when you foresee congested traffic (i.e. problems). It allows you to prepare yourself mentally with pragmatic thought of positivity tackling any issues one may face, rather than thinking the worst and aiming for disaster. Every time you feel any negative emotion or thought just say to yourself STOP

55

Silence breeds thoughts of clarity allowing circumspection of the subconscious

Think for the better, not for the worse because it is free but costly if you neglect golden positive thoughts which can help your state of mind

Of the greatest abilities known to mankind, self-control of the mind is number one

Positivity brings about nothing but good and promotes numerous benefits psychologically eventually even manifesting into ones reality. The greatest skill in life is mind-control through adopting positivity (i.e. optimism).

DIAL

Dial is an acronym used to aid train of thought, which I manifested through prison as I realized I ruminate and over think way too much. Prison systems in the year 2019 in the UK introduced 'cell-phones' to reduce mental health issues and psychological well-being. Every time a prisoner feels down or 'negative' they have the ability to contact a loved or friend through a number they DIAL.

Every time I called some soon I would feel even more down soaking my mind up with thoughts that do not serve a healthy state of mind, as I miss family, home and freedom. I molded the word DIAL into an acronym to transmit a red warning light n my mind to stay away from negative thoughts I was dialing upon, because just like the 'cell-phone' that allows you to DIAL a number than your mind too can DIAL upon thoughts of negativity or positivity, which ethers harms or benefits your mind-set.

DIAL s to ether DIAL upon one or the other and this is known as 'binary thinking'. Binary is the process of involving two things allowing options such as: heat and cold, love and hate, male and female, night and day, awake and sleep or negative and positive etc. There is an endless list as we live in a world of duality.

Having already elucidated the functions of the sub-conscious mind and its influence, the primary thesis of the mind-control is autosuggestion or as psychologist name it 'self-suggestion'. Therefore, I introduce effective acronyms self-suggesting positive thoughts as it does not strain the mind and is easy to remember as a mnemonic technique. This allows preparation of the self to have the ability to control the deepest depths of the mind.

Embracing positivity is a life-long psychological battle. Anything favourable in life consists of hard work and it is not an easy path. World record boxing champion Floyd Mayweather's career is testimony to this fact as he often cheekily remarks:" hard work is easy work". If one has to constantly maintain their physique through weight training sessions, then the same goes for the maintenance of the mind it must embrace positive thoughts (i.e. self-suggestion).

Positivity and negativity are binary options within our thoughts. They are hostile towards each other. Where one exists, the other cannot be found. Where one is resident, the other is homeless. One or the other must be dominant and this solely is determined by your discretion or train of thought.

It is for this reason I introduce effective short simple acronyms as a train of thought, if not assisting your thought process. Thoughts are either for you or against you. Thoughts are split into either one of the two categories of negative or positive, hence it is known as a way binary thinking process.

Negative Thoughts

Rumination is like a hamster wheel of doom with spinning thoughts of what could have, should have and would have been. Thinking of the past and 'what could have been' is a thought which is to be avoided. It is a psychological damaging thought almost like mental self-harm to the mind. Rumination is to bring up better matters of the past that cannot be changed. Those who indulge in this impute their own intellect, as it is foolish and the past is historic and cannot be re-written. It is a fact that blowing air from your mouth towards the sun cannot extinguish its light, so in the same way one displays a deficiency in their train of thought by continuing to ruminate knowing it cannot change anything, my point is rumination is of no positive effect whatsoever. Rumination is a roundabout going round and round wasting the fuel of thought plus your time.

Procrastination is strongly linked to rumination, as it makes the mind perceive tasks to be difficult as one fall's into a state of hopelessness. Thoughts such as: ' I don't see the point', 'I've ruined my life', 'I wish could change how I was etc'.

Generally, they are related to the past, which is a recess of the mind but useless. One generally postpones action as they are in a mental state of dither, uncertainty and become indecisive due to idleness. Procrastination wastes that which is precious and invaluable (i.e. time). Procrastination is like an open top of water dripping and each drop is like a second being wasted falling into the drain, which cannot be recovered. It nibbles away at your mind making one become useless.

Pessimism is to be negative. Pessimistic is the relative of negativity. It is to have a lack of hope or confidence about the future. Leave the future along for it is unknown. Contemplation of what is to be is just as crazy as hoping to change the past and we know this is just as crazy as hoping to change the past and we know this is impossible. When problems appear do not dwell on the issue, but find a solution. When it rains, you use an umbrella. As it is well known and said: "do not cry over spilt milk" – you just mop it up and move on. Be gentle with your mind's thoughts for it is sensitive. Do not take the harsh approach of what is to be. Worrying about what may or may not happen is of no use and sometimes beyond our control which is something you will soon come to learn or accept in your life through experiences.

Positive Thoughts
Gratitude is attitude and attitude is life. Gratitude is a state of mind, which can be cultivated. Being grateful is the key to maintenance of a healthy mind. Be grateful for a little and you have a lot. Be thankful for the past which allowed you to live to the present.

Gratitude got me through over eight rough years in prison. It completely changed my perception in life. Being thankful shifts your attention away from negativity towards positivity, and one of the great fruits of positivity is that it begets positivity.

I once read:
"those who are not thankful for little will not be thankful for a lot"

Think positive, feel positive and do positive. Think great, feel great and do great. Perfect your mental health to its utmost you possibly can through adopting the attitude of gratitude. Be grateful even if it be just for your eyes which allow you to grasp life's beauty and nature.

Gratitude Exercise
A gratitude exercise I would often do in prison is close my eyes for 10 seconds under the face of experiencing how a blind person feels, then I would open them and instantly appreciate my eyesight. This always increases my levels of gratitude. I once read a quote on instagram: *"I was crying because I could not afford new trainers than I met a man with no feet"*. The moral of this is that when a wise man once said: *"look at those inferior to you and not superior. So that you may be grateful"*. Meaning, one would realise how fortunate or thankful they are when they reverse their situation realizing it is not as bad as they thought in their mind, especially when they are familiar with those less fortunate. Not to say be happy that they are not like that, but to appreciate the thought process that 'things could have been worse'. One would this mentality is someone who always looks on the bright side even in the darkest

61

situations like facing years in prison.

I stress, we should not be happy at the less fortunate persons downfall, but realise our circumstance in comparison thereby generating gratitude, because in life there will always be someone above us doing better and someone below us doing worse. Contentment is gratitude and vice versa.

Reflection can be positive when looking back to seek inspiration. This is sensible when one understands their own value, plus reflects and seizes moments of achievement from the past to use as self-determination. This in thinking coupled along with motivating encouragement. On the other hand, looking back (at negative things) can cause you to trip moving forward.

Know that life moves on and so should you. If you are to look back, then look back at the positive highlights of your life to fuel more positive self-imagery. Being reflective is constructive thinking in the manner described. Even if you can't but think of the negative moments, then also realise those negative moments did not defeat you and you are still here today which shows a real resilience about you!

Being reflective is constructive thinking in this manner. Somewhere in the back of our mind are past thoughts, which can be a positive recess. Thoughts or moments that have gone by can be dug up to serve a positive purpose in the present or future. There is nothing wrong with searching for good in the past as a lesson to be repeated for the better.

Optimism is positivity. In fact, it is the opposite of pessimism. Optimistic is the relative of positive. It is to be hopeful or confident about an event or something in the nearby future. Humans have the tendency to be prudent and think about tomorrow in today, yet what determines tomorrow is today. Be concerned with today just as you would be when thinking of tomorrow. Hope is fundamental to aspiration. If you do not believe in yourself, be sure that nobody else will. Humans should be as ambitious as a human can be. Adopt practical plans with thought, remain optimistic and apply action of persistence. This way you segregate yourself from the idle and boot out wishful thinking. All the mind needs is the slightest iota of hope and this psychological torch enlightens the mind.

Negative Thoughts vs Positive Thoughts
This is an epitome of binary thinking where it is: optimism vs pessimism, reflection vs rumination or gratitude vs procrastination. The mind is always in an active state of chasing either one or the other, but you have the power to volunteer any thought you wish by selection of self-suggestion and electing this thought of positivity consistently until it dominates the subconscious and conscious mind. When positive thoughts strengthen; negative thoughts weaken, where positive thoughts prevail; negative thoughts do

not avail. After acknowledging all this it is only the foolish that expunge positivity at the cost of negativity, there change the thoughts you DIAL.

Change the DIAL
A dial is a feature used to select a specific purpose. For example, when one dials a number or a dial on a thermostat used to change the binary option between hot and cold. Overall, it is a selective feature and within the contents of this book it is a psychological selective indicator to adopt either positivity or negativity, but the purpose should be to always 'change the dial' to positivity away from negativity. The acronym I created to aid my thought process with DIAL actually represents:

Don't Invite Any Lament

Don't Invite Any Lament (DIAL) generally means to only dial and draw upon positive thoughts; yet at the same time avoiding any form of invitation paving a way to lament such as: regret, grief, sorrow etc because it is awfully negative and if are to be awful than be positively awful with a PLAN!

Don't pay negativity attention, the more you pay something attention, the more you feel it and it grows. Don't resist feeling negative; just shift your attention to that positive vibe which will beget more positivity eventually.

Invite negativity and you are giving indirect permission for it to reside in your mind rent-free with no purpose being served. It nibbles away at your subconscious leaving one to feel feeble.

Anything should be done to block out negativity and the same goes for your surroundings.

Lament is expressing emotion specifically grief and negativity is grievous. Manipulate feelings through change of thought or activity.

PLAN

In life our minds are always scanning for plans subconsciously with or without one's permission,
sometimes we are aware and other times we are not.
A plan is to believe and achieve. If thou believe it....
thou can achieve it. Belief including self-belief is a
strong prerequisite for one's aims to be achieved. It
is nothing but a state of mind inculcated within every
human since birth.

The mythical toothfairy is a fabricated tale famous
amongst parents and children. You know leaving your
tooth under your pillow, then you awake to money left
under your pillow supposedly from the toothfairy as a
token. Some children believe it to the extent where
they even try to pull out their own teeth, in order to
receive a token in return. Such high belief a child
possesses! They believe they can achieve without
even witnessing firsthand a 'toothfairy'.

One may present the argument that when young our
mind is ripe and receptive to anything, yet this is
positive news and evidence that we can train our
minds to believe anything we perceive just as when we
were children once upon a time.

The outcome to trick the mind is like a placebo
effect is indeed effacious to one's mental state, so
one may convince their self to achieve their plans.
With such high faith resonated in one's mindset – it
gives opportunity or the makeshift possibility to any
reasonable practical or mental achievement. Most

people that believe something is possible to any reasonable practical or mental achievement.

Most people that believe something is possible to achieve know confidently it is all within the mind. A mental battle succeeded within is indeed half the battle won already, for obtaining plans is a battle in itself requiring mental or physical action. Overall, an idea is like its name just an 'idea' – *'a thought or suggestion about a possible course of action'.* If plan had another name it would be called idea.

I am not stating in a crazy way that anything is possible and that humans can grow wings to fly, rather what I mean is if you accept the existence of something to be true, then there is no reason why you cannot achieve it through a sound practical plan. To plan is to be positive giving one a purpose in life. Know your plans can be attained, especially if someone somewhere else has already achieved alike because this means your plans are realistic and very much do exist. The mental state is the only biggest barrier between you and your plans. Often people allow even a single echo of doubt to creep in their thoughts and sway their mind, this is known as negative connotations.

If you felt extremely tired, you wouldn't prepare yourself by adoring yourself as if you were ready to attend a party on a late night. In fact, you would do the complete opposite by preparing yourself for bed, meaning you would take the correct course of action

67

appropriate to achieve a simple aim like going to sleep. Therefore, when negativity casts your judgment about your ability to 'believe and achieve' – you the complete opposite by planting positivity, as this would be the most appropriate action.

Positivity is imperative to belief in your plans, as positivity begets positivity. Behind any suggestion, idea, goal, aim or plan – it is positivity rescuing one away from negativity towards incessant hope sealing their goals in life. Positivity is coal to an old-fashioned train on route to achievement. Positivity is fuel to a car, believing is the steering wheel guiding you and the destination is success in attainment of your plans.

Positivity gets rid of the one with an inert state allowing them to believe and achieve. Positivity is the key to opening the door to achievement. Positivity is ever so bumptious because it can be hard to grasp mentally especially for those who face their lowest ebbs in life. You struggle to be positive surrounded by negativity especially when you cannot help but think negative as you feel hopeless with 'no light at the end of the tunnel'.

In these moments nothing seems to be going good for yourself in life. Along comes a person who you despise, yet for some weird reason you still seem to be acquainted with and they advise: 'you need to be positive', yet these words coming from their mouth to your ear have never been so irritating, but this exact mentality is one of malice, rancor and most of all negative. Give positivity a try, what have you got to lose – nothing, yet everything to possibly gain.

One of the fruits of positivity is that it pregnates even more positivity, whereas one of the bitter aspects of negativity is that it invites more negativity. Every single person breathing is in need of positivity. Your mind is a garden and you must plant seeds of positivity.

The worst is not to come but the best is. There is light at the end of the tunnel. If you hit rock bottom; the only way is up. Even a blind man can see how great positivity is with its numerous beneficial effects.

Positivity, purpose, plan coupled along with action make an irresistible set of characteristics healthy for the mind. Know that being positive, having a purpose and plan is great but they are all useless when not infused with action.

Plan without action is like a gun without ammunition or a car without fuel.... it becomes stale and useless. It just looks great and eye-pleasing, no different from a wishful thinker. Action itself with no end aim however is also useless. Action is the process of exerting effort to do something. Action (work) is the bridge between visualisation and reality.

Thoughts, ideas and plans are just a mental impression – whereas effort, labour and action are physical impressions. Mental mirrors physical, hence continual state of action gets desired results. If one remains physically depressed, then his physical state mirrors this by being idle and this is a known fact. On the other hand, positivity is to be motivated, ambitious and determined as you can possibly be, which will take shape in its physical counterpart sooner rather than later.

At the core of action is persistence, meaning persistence to plan is just as important as what the heart is to the body. Persistence gets you what you want. Commonly, when drenched in negativity the mental problems people have is lack of ambition, hope, and this makes one dither with their aims living an indecisive lifestyle. Generally, they live in a state of confusion as it seems like to their self and others they know what they are doing but in reality they have very little figured out. On the other side of things, one who has a sound plan backed with active persistence is like an arrow that does not miss its target in sight.

Even if you took it upon yourself to do a self-study project involving a mini research of just asking fifty different people – what they want most out of life or what their purpose is – many would struggle to tell you. If you really them for a response, some will say power and fame, most will say abundance of money (i.e. to be rich), while others with mediocrity will

70

commonly say a 'comfortable' life whatever that means and only a minority will mention the sole expedition of peace and contentment, which is almost scarce in today's world. Seldom do people mention religion, heaven, hell or an afterlife. The noteworthy point here, is not knowing what you want, not having a plan leads usually to a derelict unsettled life. Whereas, any goal or aim in life responds to purpose, action, persistence all smothered in a plan.

To plan is to be ambitious. Being ambitious does not always mean to strive for the 'bigger, greater' things in life, there is no wrong in living a mediocre life proving that's what you truly plan for yourself. I have lived years in prison living a simple life and plan to continue this way of simplicity even upon release. That is my entitlement of ambition, and you have one too, which is down to your sole discretion or choice.

Ambition is what elevates ones thought process to be determined to succeed their plans. It is a strong desire to achieve something. Ambition is the yacht that glides smoothly in the ocean of desire allowing one to appropriately reach their destination when the time is right. Ambition is fuel to attain your goal or the accomplishment of your plans.

If ambition could be defined in another way it would be: 'a strong reason why'. Scientific research and psychologists state that a 'purpose-driven' life (i.e. a strong reason why) offers tranquility to the mind and solidarity strengthening one's mind frame.

Live by purpose, not idleness. Every human is the perfect candidate to contain a 'strong reason why' to achieve their aims in life. This is also strongly linked with motivation and determination, both essential to your plans in life. Be clear what your ambitions are and believe in yourself that you can achieve them.

When one is truly introduced to ambition and welcomes it, then it allows opportunity to flow into every corner of your mind effortlessly. Ambition soaks up positivity in the same way a sponge absorbs water. Ambition is like a vehicle steering you closer towards your desired destination (i.e. plans and goals). Amongst this pathway is a road named 'Problem Avenue', for if life had another name it would be called problematic. Therefore, one should have an attitude of solubility, regardless of what issues you may come across in life.

Man With A Plan
For the ease of the writer being male himself, he refers to this section as 'man with a plan'; simply for the ease of the authors experience himself. In no way shape or form is he being prejudice or sexist in this part of the chapter. Every part within this book equally applies to woman just as much.

A man's ambition is a great tool of his life. This is because any person who possesses high ambitions will select the highest goals. They will attempt to reach this pinnacle but the possibility that it may be a race against time (i.e. death is inevitable) as they are gifted with a limited unknown time or that his access to opportunities is insufficient.

Remaining aplomb is a must, for panic brings no good. Understanding yourself is just as important as knowing your plans. You are your plans and your plans are you. With that being said, one should understand that amongst every human the three innate traits of lust, anger and intellect. Among these inborn characteristics one is always leading further than the other. All three reside within the mind, therefore making your mind like a driver and your body like a vehicle which transmits towards one's goals. Overall, one should ensure his inner self, referred to as the 'lingual self' often is dominant and lets this trait lead him over the other two.

The advice of this is because the human culture is innately familiar with good and bad. Everything is distinguished by something and intellect is the distinction of human. Therefore, we should use this characteristic to be thoughtful about our plans in life and act accordingly. On the other hand, are those who do not contemplate or they may but it is nothing more than drifting thoughts that manifest into nothing. Their target is nothing and they accurately achieve it, as they are intimidated by failure.

Winners or goal achievers are very well acquainted with defeat and see it as something temporary to learn from or a hurdle to get over. Generally, they know that 'my plans go to plan when they do not go to plan', because things in life do not always happen specifically as you may have thought or planned in your head. Be sure to meet with obstacles, but treat them like hurdles you must overcome or hop over. Your job is to remain persistent, have self-belief, and remain positive. Know your purpose and strive with continuous effort. Remember 'fail to plan and you plan to fail'. This is a very important principle in life.

Many act and exert effort because they have to (i.e. responsibility) – known as forced action as people (i.e. family) are dependent upon them. Yet, a simple shift in thought completely changes this scenario, instead of feeling burdened with responsibility. You should take this positively with gratitude and purpose. One should be joyous filled with exuberant energy knowing their purpose is their family, which is sufficient. This triggers motivation rather than being burdened, a positive mind frame.

Apart of the package of plans is to know what you want and have the determination to succeed. It can be described as an obsession dominated by a plan with purpose. You choose a goal or goals that you definitely want and exert all effort, energy and willpower into achieving it.

You are the perfect candidate for leading your life and steering it in your favour. Convince yourself with ease that you will do what it takes to acquire your plans to be fulfilled.

Plans are filled in a parcel with desire, state of mind, obsession, persistence, ambition, motivation, determination along with action otherwise you may fall into the category of a 'wishful thinker'. When you have plans it allows you to be self-reliant with the golden ability to believe and achieve. You should make planning become a self-formed habit beginning with a 'to-do list' and more importantly in life. A family of idea, faith, plan, action, decision, thought habits and persistence are all relatives to achievement.

Ideas and plans are akin to each other. Where there is a will, there is a way. A plan is a single step forward that will crystalise or animate into your reality. Apart of your plans should also be to throw off any negativity whether that be environment, company or activities that may influence you. Nothing should stand in your way, not even your own sceptism or doubt, so long as you apply suitability of hard work being practical. Your plan should always be to stick to the plan. If something goes wrong re-evaluate your plan to get to the plan – this is what is known as 'plan b', or 'plan c' or 'plan d' etc. This is also called persistence when you rebuild your plans.

You should *plan your work, then work your plan.*

I once read:
"When Plan A fails, there is 26 letters left"!

Keep it simple, even if you make slow progress because slow progress is better than no progress. Choose what you require, create a sound plan and exert practical action with consistency, for this is the epitome of persistence. Focus and concentrate, butcher any distractions.

When a marathon runner jogs they do not exert all their energy lest they be drained; they take a pragmatic approach being consistent so that they may achieve their end goal. This is the example of persistence of one planning their goals.

Cultivation of persistence is to strengthen your state of mind in accordance with your set-goals overseen by consistent planning backed by action. Desire is powerful and it is at the core of one's plans. Desire is to know what you want and this is vital to mental growth plus development. You can start off with something as simple as a 'to-do list'.

Making a 'to-do list' is a good technique to break down your goals by creating sub-goals acting as pigeon steps or slow progress towards the major goal. Create a list and tackle each agenda beginning with the easiest task first, as this allows you to work your through consistently. It uplifts your thought, mood and feeling eventually building self-confidence.

Humans are incentive creatures and having a plan allows one to tug on to a motive that can overcome obstacles. One's plans should be reasonable, practical and well-organised. It is imperative to be partnered with continuous effort.

Another day, another opportunity. Every day is a fresh opportunity to put your plan into action. You will face challenges but these help you grow, regardless of what may have been thrown in your pathway – you must remain resilient by sticking to the plan. Let the plan become your 'strong reason why' to spur you on in moments of struggle. Make it happen!

Goals are a desired result, and results are achieved through planning with many quality traits whether it be persistence, organisation, patience, resilience, awareness, effort, ambition but all over shadowed by a plan because it rids of any mental astigmatism (i.e. negativity) paving a way to your goals!

Get Objective Aims Lucidly Setup

Get familiar with yourself knowing what you want

Objectives build constant momentum and can be viewed as a positive catalyst.

Aim at your objectives with a target called 'action'

Lucidity allows maintaining simplicity towards goals

Setup your plans or goals instantly, do not procrastinate. This is the first step to achievement.

SELF

There is nothing more important to self than the self. You without yourself cannot function. Mans biggest or greatest asset is man (or women too). To take care of life and to take care of yourself. In yourself there is a self you must take care of and that is your self-suggestive thoughts. As already elucidated on page 57, thoughts are binary either positive or negative and the same applies to self-suggestion. A man can drive himself crazy with his thoughts or drive himself to success in achieving whatever it is they may desire from this journey named life.

Studying yourself allows you to acknowledge your strengths and weaknesses that ultimately enriches your inner self (i.e. mind) and widens the scope of your faculties. To acknowledge is knowledge and knowledge to the mind is like a tread mill for the body, meaning it exercises your brain through stimulation of your mind. Your mind is a deposit bank and like any bank you should only accept valuable items, in this sense that would be useful suggestions. This deposition makes your thoughts become mental jewels serving wellness into your life.

The criteria to build one's character can only be done through mastering the self. It is to indoctrinate your thoughts not allowing yourself to become susceptible to your circumstance, environment, company or a victim of your negative thoughts. You have to hypnotize yourself by control of thought as if you are in a form of trance unaware of your surroundings. In short, brainwash yourself or be brainwashed by the condition of your environment and surroundings.

I could have easily become mad in prison serving nearly a decade, witnessing violence, the noises, even the smell, sometimes I think I am mad till today most people today call it 'tapped', but I like to think I tried my best to cling onto fortitude via self-suggestion. It allowed me to stay focused and become an author and write all these books along with other projects I am working on. I had my ups and down in prisons but it comes with it and at the end of the day all that matters to myself is myself.

The mind is hostile, if not tamed can be a very intricate place often hard to comprehend when confused with emotion. From the onset let's make one thing clear segregate emotion from thought and thought from emotion. Do not let your feelings do the thinking for you; otherwise this is the same as letting someone else think for you. If you are to mix thought with feeling, then adopt synchronicity.

You can synchronise your emotions with your thinking to serve you in your favour, if you cannot eradicate or segregate the pair. When positively combined thought and emotion can be an unstoppable force.

This can be achieved through persistent self-scrutiny. Take into consideration your every thought and feeling to manipulate them in order to sway in your favour, rather than halt you or delay progress.

The trick is to adopt introspection on a regular basis and investigate yourself through question and answer. Making a 'thoughts journal' is a great solution. Consistently have conversations in your head and jot them down, why are you feeling or thinking the way you are. The more you scrutinise, the more you challenge your subconscious, the more understanding the more control. Your mind will work with you rather than against you. This is an example of how to train your mind to work in benefit with you.

Observation allows understanding of the details in your mind. As stated on page 35 'the best conversations in life are the silent ones in our head' and this is exactly what I meant by it. You are thinking about the way you think and many philosophers plus psychologists label this as 'intelligent thought' or 'powerful thinking'. Napoleon Hill once shared there was a friend of his who had a dark room with a lamp, desk, chair, paper and pen – it was the only stationary in his office which would help him think.

Observe yourself for it only brings good. Knowing yourself allows comfortability in one's mind and rid of any influence of environment or company. It allows you to accumulate experience and shift perspective. This allows a negative to be molded into a positive. For example, many famously say that this experience was 'a blessing in disguise', because they observe their thoughts and circumstance before; in comparison to now, which they can derive a lesson from that they may have not necessarily gained any other way (i.e. hindsight). This is all through positive reflection, observation and scrutiny. That happened for a reason and that reason taught me to keep going no matter what. This builds fortitude and resilience, but can only be achieved through 'self-suggestion'.

In other words, self-suggestion is when the mind conversates with the subconscious mind. You can instruct your mind to only adopt thoughts that bring about positivity. Nothing is a barrier when it comes to tricking your mind to believe what you want it to believe. Every thought in your head can be erased or replaced like a document in a cabinet file. You give every thought a meaning and can suggest what you will whether it empowers you or not.

"Every thought is an investment or a cost"

Voluntary injection into the subconscious mind cultivates mind-control. When I mention inner self, I mean and refer to the subconscious mind that is deeply rooted in the mind. Domination of the mind is achieved through voluntarily suggesting what you please consistently. This is the beauty of willpower and what we humans are distinguished by.

You choose whether your thought or feeling match either positive or negative and you encourage or discourage both until they synchronise to your benefit. This allows control and elimination, control of positive thoughts and elimination of negativity.

This state of mind can only be achieved through the mother of indoctrination, which is repetition. When anything is repeated enough it becomes deeply rooted not just in the mind, but the subconscious until one eventually acts upon these self-ingrained thoughts. Before you know it your mind becomes dominated and so much so that you may not be able to eradicate your positive train of thought. Even when faced with harsh situations, you naturally remain optimistic and others define this as insane, but insanity is not to control your own mind and thoughts.

Why this is so, simply because of a self-formed habit. In fact, habits are known to be one of human's strongest disposition because we are creatures of habit and mind-control (in this sense 'self-suggestive positive thoughts') is attained through persistence of habit. Hence, create thought habits.

Disposition over circumstance, not circumstance over disposition. You can become the hero of your own storey or a victim of circumstance simply through your thought. You become what you dominantly think as you breed self-belief. The lexical equivalent of this is to say that any thought continually repeated worms its way into the subconscious until it is believed, accepted and finally acted upon.

An epitome just like I mentioned on page 20 is Cristiano Roanldo; one of the world's greatest footballers ever. When Piers Morgan interviewed the football legend and asked 'how he achieved his dreams?', Cristiano pointed towards his head and said 'it's in my mind'. He chose disposition over circumstance, had he wanted he could have easily made himself believe he was given a star role for a movie named 'another sob story in life' because he grew up in poverty, yet he we adopted fortitude, resilience and strength through a repetitive positive train of thought. He always told himself that he wanted to be the best and he became the best, winning many trophies and awards.

Many successful people understand well to achieve your aims whether small or large can be done with ease through repetition of thought firmly situated in one's mind. Repeating a purposeful definite aim gives one that drive they need to build positivity and throws away negativity in any form it appears. Arouse your thoughts through observation and it elevates your scope of thinking to heights that really allow you to see things in life for what they really are and a much more beautiful perspective giving one belief and hope to accomplish their goals.

Create thought habits with acronyms revealed in this book like 'STOP' on page 56 or 'DIAL' on page 65. These acronyms serve your conscious faculty and administer your train of thought due to it having an easy memorization (i.e. mnemonic technique) process with repetition to ingrain within your sub-conscious that can achieve what you think you couldn't.

Self-suggestion Equals Lenient Fortitude

Self-suggestion is mental preparation to coerce the deepest depths of your mind to work in your favour.

Equating into eventual action in reality shaping one's life through achievement of plans, ideas and goals

Leniency is the best approach for the mind for it is fragile and must be handled with care

Fortitude is the end product making one's self resilient with the greatest quality mind-control

Continually suggesting to yourself to build mental strength to live a favourable life is fortitude and controlling one's self. Intelligent and successful people know full well the development of the mind is the greatest value. One can create his own world in his head and reside in it without gaining any riches, he may be viewed as mad but to himself he knows he had achieved what he always wanted without the flick of a muscle and this is referred to as 'peace of mind'.

Fortitude through faculty. You behave as you think. Whatever your major goal, aim, plan, idea or purpose in life can only be acquired through knowledge, and thought well thought is like a sponge that absorbs allowing you to acknowledge. Thought is a sponge that never dries up, therefore we should use it to soak up as much as knowledge as we can relative to our purpose-driven life.

Self is to rely on yourself, otherwise known as self-reliance. When you truly adopt the ways of self-suggestion, your priorities are set straight and you only rely on your thoughts that you have carefully curated to serve your aim. Everything else becomes irrelevant allowing self-reliance to truly manifest. Within the self is as many 'self's' as you wish, there is self-reliance, self-belief, self-taught, self-confidence, self-planned, self-fortitude, self-determination, self-motivated and the list goes on but this can only be achieved through mastery of the self (i.e. mind control of the subconscious).

Let introspection become a life-long habit control your mind and more importantly your life.

Control your mind; do not let your mind control you

I am a strong believer in God and strongly feel that this divine prerogative of though (i.e. willpower) is to aid humans to strive to be the best beings we possibly can to living in harmony amongst one another. Your character is a mirrored reflection of yourself, which can be molded through the effective psychological principle of self-suggestion.

Self-analysis is at the fundamental core of control of the mind, willpower, freewill and train of thought. Self-analysis is introspection, whereby one examines one's thoughts and feelings altering their state of mind continuously throughout life, even after one's aims one achieved because knowledge is endless. You can never be a 'know-it-all', where there are so many you have not learnt. Be a 'learn-it-all', not a 'know-it-all' and this is something I learnt in prison. Often when prisoners conversate, I realised these words frequently 'yeah, I know that', but I vowed to myself I will be a learner not a knower. I would rather say 'yeah, I learnt that' & I refuse to stop learning. Invest in yourself through learning, learn who you are, learn what you want, learn from others around you and learn life itself. This is how you take care of the self.

87

DR PEPPER

Dr Pepper is not an actual doctor if such but more of a brand and to be precise a well-known can drink. That's right! Dr Pepper is a cola brand and this chapter is based on its advertisement, with a strong moral question:

"What's The Worst That Could Happen?"

If you have ever seen the advert you will know exactly what I'm talking about. Mostly at the end of the advertisement often the following slogan is displayed. My point is this slogan is a positive question to foster for your mentality when faced with doom and gloom.

The slogan itself promotes an optimistic attitude when we find our self in a dark pit of anguish, grief and stress. What is the worst that can happen, surely it can only get better from here and often chances are you can bounce back from the situation. Besides there is no point in pondering over what is useless, so leave the future alone for it is unknown. One can ruminate until their head is spinning with thoughts but this will only leave their sense dizzy and confused. Do not think too hard, take matters easy and this way you will not find your affairs scattered.

Life is such that it is like this, that may happen what you wish and you need to do this or this may happen what you wish, then you need to do that. There is a time for this and there is a time for that. Life is hard, so be easy on yourself. Know that life never pans out how you want because it is unpredictable. The most affluent or successful people will tell you how many hurdles they had to hope over or the amount of barriers they had to overcome before finally getting to their destination.

Be sure that everyone meets turmoil in life and this is inevitable. Many people have been robbed of their ability to either hold or enjoy their wealth, possessions or fortune through no fault of their own. The same man that rose to fame in an instance was only years later found to be publicly disgraced and vilified in the media. The same man who accumulated riches, years later lost it all and it was as if he had never tasted such wealth. This is life. A man may be affluent overnight due to an idea springing to mind which he manifested into a global selling product, then overnight became a pauper due to a financial crash or even a wrong investment decision. My point is do not be extremely happy in times of joy and do not despair too much in times of grief. Be moderate, take your matters easy, be humble, be kind, be you!

It is only those with half-baked brains that do not understand one must meet with failure several times before arriving at the location of success. It is a rollercoaster ride with twists, turns and bends which you do not know is around the corner or may not hold. Positivity is a ladder, which elevates one's position towards their aim, whereas negativity is a heavy mental burden that can weigh you down often leaving

89

one stuck in a rut or in stale in life.

Life is all about progression and learning. This is something I have learnt in my years being alive. Each day that goes by is a brand new packaged opportunity to progress and be different from what yesterday was. Your mind is like a remote, which you have the power to control. I really want you to read, meditate and think as you read to soak up the information in this book for it is your benefit.

Everyone has to pass the test of persistence to get where they want and there is no other path or shortcuts in life. Even if you are making slow progress in the right direction one step at a time, then that is great. You have to keep moving, even by crawling. You can become your own since personal advisor through fortitude and self-value which is of immeasurable value itself. As I stated on page 35: *'the best conversations in life are the silent one's that we hold in our head'*, as silence breeds priority plus clarity. Original wisdom can be gained silence, humbleness and modesty.

Humans race to seek that, which benefits their self first. With that being stated it is solely your choice to help yourself. You have a mind of your own with original thoughts. Use your mind to reach prompt decision. You know I mention thinking so much and it is because I am a professional thinker as in prison all I could do was think and think and think and think.

I adopted a mind habit of power thinking. So I began to jot my thoughts down transforming them into many books and projects, not just one but many I can honestly say I never imagined or planned to ever be an author, but it is something I enjoy. Sometimes I think it was a fluke or just happened, but soon realised it I am going through an experience and it can be shared which is unique. Many people are introduced to an unknown talent of theirs often when met with some sort of crisis and mine happened to be when I was spending years in prison.

It is important to remember 'life is to overcome constant failure'. You have to fail to achieve but never achieve to fail. Possibly even multiple times you may fail, but this is just the pathway to achieving one's aim, goal or purpose in life. Be sure to meet with many misfortunes. This is a prerequisite for success.

You have to arm yourself with patience, fortitude, courage and a solid impenetrable mind shut off against any discouraging influences whether that is someone or something. Focus on your mentality for it transports you places the body could never take you. I have suffered mental health problems and this is why the theme of the book is strongly shaped on the subject of the mind. I share my experience or tips that I have to offer, which helped me overcome some of these misfortunes I faced in life, as life is what you are and you are your mentality because mentality is nothing but a train of thought or a way of thinking. It is all about your perspective of life.

91

MENTAL HEALTH

Our mental state is sensitive, so be gentle and cautious. Many people brush aside mental well-being solely focusing on their physical state, but if anything the mind should be nurtured more. Having awareness of your mental health and developing your mindset is a blessing of priority. One who has a 'strong head on their shoulders' or 'their head screwed on', usually means someone who has good mental health allowing them to generally to think, feel and react appropriately in the ways required to live your life.

When experiencing mental health issues it can be disruptive and bewildering. You may feel down and it becomes an invisible barrier between achieving your aims, for everything or anything that manifests originates from the mind. Mental health affects roughly around one in four people, and can be sometimes be nothing but a misconception hugged with negative thought. We may 'fear the worst' which is totally non-existent and unrealistic at times, but for the one who suffers may not be able to broaden his horizons to rise above the surface to see different or think differently. This can leave one drenched in a negative mind frame increasing anxiety or grief paving a way to isolation.

There is a big big confusion between mental health and emotional well-being because some may think they are not relative to one another but this is incorrect as thoughts effect directly the way we feel and the way we feel has a parallel result on our thinking process. It is unknown in history of a personal feeling happy, yet committed suicide unless they was seeking martyrdom, but my point is cognitive behaviour is a result of thought, then feeling, then action or feeling, then thought and then action.

Understanding is important for it is the cure to ignorance and a stop towards self-education. Having a cultural religious background helps deal with one's mental state and emotions. The way you think and feel are closely associated and are of the same. Different ideologies are practical for different beliefs determined by one's mentality or traditions.

Having spent years upon years in prison, I have come across and interacted with many people from different walkways of life that I may have never necessarily come across in the outside world. I always saw this an opportunity to seek wisdom and learn something, as it can widen one's insight. Time and again in life we encounter men and women who state how they feel and this is because the way we feel is a receipt of our thoughts. Have you ever heard anyone say "I'm thinking down", because I haven't. This is because emotions are surfacing all the time, whereas you have to dig a little deeper to discover the status of your thought process.

Poor emotional health is no different from poor mental well-being. Same concept, just different words. Illness is to be ill and to be ill is simply not in good health whether that be mental or physical, because health is a condition of both mental and physical.

Just as there are so many different physical illnesses the same applies for mental diseases. Thinking is a diagnosis especially with issues within the mind. Feelings is a symptom of what is going on mentally within one's head. Therefore, one could suffer more than one symptom or discover more than one issue through diagnosis just as they body may be stricken with illnesses simultaneously. Here are some of the most common health problems:

Phobias
Everything has an extreme and phobia to have extreme fear of something for a long period, which can be caused by a specific scenario or item, even though there is no threat. This could be spiders or one bad event a person experienced which triggered them to not go outside anymore. Generally, a fear is an unpleasant emotion caused by a threat or danger but fear evolves into phobia when the danger or threat becomes melodramatic, yet it cannot be taken lightly as for some it ruins their social life having a major impact on their daily life.

OCD (Obsessive Compulsive Disorder)
There are many types of anxiety disorders and OCD is one of them. There is a huge misconception that OCD is only linked to being extremely clean, organised and tidy, but this is not true. It is a illness,

which can be tricky to comprehend. It is divided into two categories as below:
Obsession – being continually attached to stress, doubt, worry or negative thoughts that are constantly self-suggestive to the mind.
Compulsion – activities or events you feel you must do to reduce anxious state triggered by the obsession in your mind.

Anxiety
Trepidation is another name for anxiety. The identification of anxiety is the way we feel – this may be when we are nervous, afraid or worried especially linked with possible future outcomes. Being prudent can be a cause of anxiety but this is completely natural as humans have the tendency to 'forward-think', but continuous prudent thoughts for a period can make you burdened. Anxiety disorders can cause panic attacks and insomnia. Everyone has felt anxious at one point in their life, but being anxious all the time letting it consume your mind becomes a clear diagnosis for a disorder. This is determined upon the symptoms that may diagnose a specific type of anxiety. Overall, if you are mildly anxious there is nothing wrong with that because it is in our nature.

Bipolar Disorder
This is a mood-based and once known as 'manic depression'. It is to sway in-between two different episodes of feeling low (depressive episodes) and feeling high (manic or hypomanic episodes). Sometimes it may have potentially psychotic

95

symptoms. Mood swings are natural inclination of humans but bi-polar is more extreme in impacting one's life. It can be very depressing and obtuse for the one who suffers from this mental state. Overall, it is when one sways between high and low moods continuous daily.

Personality Disorder
This is a serious self-esteem based issue determined by one's behaviour, attitude, thought process and belief and it can be stemmed into life-long issues. One who diagnosed with this mental health problem may constantly have difficulties with their mentality and perspective, even if unwanted. Categorically, there are many types of personality disorder, but the two commonly diagnosed are: BPD and ASPD.
BPD is borderline personality disorder. This is strongly related to one who is emotionally unstable near an incurable extent.
ASPD is anti-social personality disorder. This is those who struggle to socialise in their life.

Schizophrenia
A fanatical mind state, which includes a withdrawal from reality is one way of describing this mental illness. Amongst its symptoms includes being reclusive, psychosis, lack of interest, irregular thought and speech, disheveled, disconnected from emotion and much more. There is a lot of confusion to the actual definition of schizophrenia itself.

Self-Harm

There is a physical form of lament, whereby one expresses their grief though harming their self. It is a unfit coping technique to deal with intricate emotion especially painful feelings or moments replaying in one's mind. Self-harm takes the succumbed person's mind away from matters temporarily, it is a short term release of trepidation and worry.

Suicide

Before action is feeling and thought, therefore suicidal feelings often derive when feels they are in their lowest ebbs in life, as a result they unsoundly conclude 'life is not worth living' or 'they cannot take anymore'. This is scary as it can go undetected and tragically lead to loss of life, if one does not talk or express their thoughts or feeling, then feeling suicidal usually comes about due to a plethora of built up thoughts or even events. For example, a child may be continually bullied feels extremely helpless, which leads to low self-esteem and sadly results in them taking their own life. Some may feel suicidal or think to commit suicide, but do not actually carry out the action (like I have many times). When you do feel suicidal and the feelings become resurgent this can be declared as an emergency and should be treated just as one who is severely bleeding, because it is life-threatening. Talk to someone.

Depression

People are divided with their opinions as in to what

depression actually is and some view it as 'absorbing reality' because some have a depressing reality. There are many misconceptions to its actual definition and terminology, for example a person may feel their life is not the best or as they like to label it 'depressing', yet true depression is a constant mental state of hopefulness and unhappiness over a long period of time. Everyone is prone to experience a depressing moment, or feel sad and hopeless at one stage in their life and yes they may feel down or 'depressed' for that moment but it fades away. Depression applies to those who mentally suffer with worthlessness everyday of their life to the point it pushes them towards being inactive and idle. They cannot function as they normally would due to their mental state of thought. Severe depression leads to self-harm and suicide.

Triggers of Mental Health Problems
There are endless factors to assess regarding one's state of mind and many issues to address before diagnosis or treating symptoms. Generally, mental health is non-physical and should be treated alike, but the roots of such causes are often too embedded within the mind. A thought deeply rooted within the mind can explode or be exaggerated leading to mental health being poor. Consecutive elements accumulated especially the way one thinks can cause colossal mental issues – a normal man/woman can be deemed mad. It is an unseen world of cause and effect, which sometimes goes undiscovered, if not spoken about.

Poor mental well-being can be triggered by factors such as:
Drug and alcohol misuse
Chronic low feelings
Homelessness
Unemployment or being poor
Bereavement
Chronic psychological illness or condition
Mental abuse in childhood (i.e. trauma or neglect)
Bullying
Domestic violence
Social isolation
PTSD (Post traumatic stress disorder)

These are primary triggers and there are many more. Most of these are associated with 'state of mind' but for some the trigger or cause could be one's physical condition such as: they suffered from falling at a height resulting in neurological damage due to the head injury, hence leading to a mental health problem or even disability like autism or epilepsy etc.

Neurological Mental Health
This relates to brain chemicals that affect our mental state due to hormones like dopamine, oxytocin and serotonin. All three have been strongly linked with social media and many users admit 'feeling rubbish' or 'low in mood' after scrolling online. There is a lot of research from experts revealing the correlation between mental health, brain chemistry and social media playing a role in being negatively

effacious to humans. This is due to a chemical imbalance synthesised by the digital compounds of social media which affect our brain chemistry. There has been precedented evidence of teenager's committing suicide and self-harming as a result of social media having an effect on their mental health.

Reason being because humans are cognitive creatures and what we see, touch or feel does have an impact on our physical as well as mental health. What we sense directly penetrates our mood, emotion and state of mind. It is a very complicated matter and some psychiatrists or doctors prescribe medicine for neurological health in order to treat it or balance out the chemicals. Studies have proven this to be true and one of the prime examples of this is CBD (endocanniboid). This is a serious issue because how can people who have poor mental health be sought help, if they their own self do not raise awareness because they suffer from low mood, thought or feeling making it even to difficult to express their emotion from the onset. When I was reading and doing research for this book I came across a magazine about mental health which mentioned a term named 'alexithymia'.

Alexithymia
This is a broad term used to describe 'problems with feeling emotions'. In fact, this Greek term used in Freudian psychodynamic theories loosely translates to 'no words for emotions'. A lot of people do say ' I don't know how I feel' which I assume could be

similar. While the condition is not well-known, it is estimated that 1 in 10 people have it.

Diagnosis of Mental Health
It is a complicated procedure but a process of the psychiatrist, doctor or mental health team to request information directly from the patient. Being inquisitive and asking questions is fundamental to understanding one's mood, behaviour and pattern of thought, so the appropriate action or treatment can be pursued. Some symptoms may appear evidently clear and this can be comprehended with ease due to the experience of the team dealing with the patient's issues. Communication is a core factor to gain as much detail as possible to help the one suffering, but it is a role to be played by both parties, for those helping and the one who needs helped.

Coping Strategies/Techniques
Care for your own self is vital to manage your physical and mental aptitude. You must think long-term because some mental health issues are ephemeral and by thinking long-term allows one to focus consistently. Self-care strategies are commonly advised by healthcare staff to prevent one's condition of exacerbating. There are various treatments for different people, some work for others and some do not. This is determined solely by the person their self and what they find to be effective such as: therapy, meditation or self-help etc. With mental health it can be cured by near enough anything reasonable that you may think is

therapeutic. Self-help such as that offered in this book can help with core principles that are strongly based around helping one's self. It may work for some and for some it may not, but it did work for me because I was locked up in prison isolated manifesting various different types of mental health issues such as: anxiety, depression and bipolar disorder, yet I had to help myself. It is a slow working progress and there is no one dose solution instantly curing anyone. It is a gradual process of recovery costing time, communication and effort. Here are a few tips on some self-help strategies:

- Awareness

Self-consciousness of your mental health is imperative as it allows you to communicate how you feel, so others may help.
When there is a dip in your feelings or evident signs, then talk about it as these serve as red flags to your state of mind.
Monitor and assess your emotions, what makes you feel the way you feel. Take notes on yourself.

- Keep Fit

Scientific research has proven exercise improves one's mental wellbeing.
Looking after your physical health nourishes your feelings (i.e. makes you feel better)
Relaxation is just as important as it can build sufficient energy to rejuvenate your mind

- Socialise

Being social allows you to be connected and possibly share your feelings lifting 'weight off your shoulders' Communicating builds self-esteem and confidence in being vocal and distributing your perspective Socialising reduces the feeling of isolation paving a way to feeling a member of society.

- Therapeutic Activities

This is anything that improves your mental state it could be sport, painting or even reading a book. Find, learn or adopt a hobby that you know helps you feel better and think clearly. Simply cherishing small activities like having a bath, shower or rest does improve mental health.

- Peer Groups

Discussion of your problems in a group allows venting and builds self-confidence Meeting new people is refreshing and your experience could help them (vice versa) An opportunity to learn something new and improve your emphatic skills.

If you feel like you are not capable of self-care techniques, then you should try to see your GP, doctor, psychiatrist or nurse to find appropriate help or treatment, but giving these self-help techniques is worth a try before seeking professional health care.

MIND OVER MATTER

'Disposition over circumstance' are three words that are substitute for 'mind over matter'. Your mind being disposition, which can overcome any matter (i.e. circumstance, scenario or situation).

Many people believe life just happens and that we have little control over the condition of events we experience, which is true to some extent but we can at times have just as much as control over our circumstances through our state of mind.

How we choose to react to these circumstances is what really matters. If you want to change condition you may find yourself in, then you must first change the condition within yourself (i.e. your mentality).

Yes, some things in life do unpredictably unfold that we cannot tame, but be sure if there is something we can control and some things we cannot; know that it is your mind. Some things we can control and some things we cannot, but freewill, power and mentality strongly shapes our perception of the situation.

If you really want to grip life by the horns, then grab self-control over your minds thoughts and feelings. It is unequivocal that feelings and thoughts are of the same – I thought and I felt – meaning he thinks the way he feels. You often hear people say: "let me have a THINK about it and see how I FEEL". It's the same.

Truth is feelings and thought are very much synchronised, where one goes the other follows like Siamese twins joint at the hip. Majority of moments in your life have been a product of your emotion and thoughts. You very much hold the key to the door of transition through feeling and thinking. You have the ability to change your life through these aptitudes. Choice, thought, feeling, action and in the end result; are all combined to manifest change in your life!

Only you have complete access to your mind and can manipulate it. Don't be so impressionable by what surrounds you and dominate your thoughts.

Humans are sensitive creatures as we have the sense of feeling, this becomes like a mental ignition to steer and drive one's life as one prefers due to the faculty of thought combined. Imperative it is to remember that they (emotion and thought) work together just like car and fuel. How thoughtless thoughts appear in the mind, yet come to nothing. So many thoughts pop up and disappear in a single day that are not acted upon, but when infused with feeling it will irresistibly transform itself into a matter or circumstance that you desired. The mixture of strong feeling with thinking usually does elicit into action. What you feel matters just as much as what you think.

EMOTIONAL INTELLIGENCE

How do we learn emotional control?

If emotion had another name it would be labeled as 'feelings of thoughts', as the two are inevitably related and cannot or will not be segregated. They are glued together to work with one another, and both have a simultaneous effect. They both dominate each other equally and as fair as fair can be. Thought being a vehicle, emotion being a fuel and consciousness being the navigator. The way we dominantly think eventually clothes itself in some form of action, the way we feel is interlinked as it behaves like an ignition and the way our conscious (i.e. our choice) allows direction to where we want to go.

All three traits could be described in two different words – ignition or impetus. It can even be given as a parable of a animal like a horse – consciousness being the rein of the horse and thought plus feeling being the horse itself. Just as one has the ability to get on and off a horse as they please, than they too can command to manipulate their thought plus emotion; changing or switching them on and off as they please.

To achieve a state of being a master over yourself and that includes controlling your innate faculties such as thinking and feeling; it requires a shift of perspective quite intelligently. You have to withdraw yourself away from yourself and be analytical. This will allow you to realise you are not your feeling and thought but actually allowed yourself to be. Now, you can choose to continue the way you think and feel or change it, because true conscious or self-awareness is the ability to choose in the present moment what you want, feel or think is best for you, regardless of the matter, situation or circumstance you may be in.

If you feel sad, you can feel happy but it is well-known that humans have been through every feeling on the emotion spectrum, and do not always act on how they feel unless it is mixed with some thought. Saying this, thought allows you to analyse and manipulate your emotion or however you feel.

"Introspection when mastered allows self mind-control, to be in full order of your thoughts"

Introspection is to examine your thought and feelings to aid the enhancement of your life. Such blessing is emotion that with going through a particular feeling it allows you to truly realise another psychological sensation (i.e. feeling). It is through being sad, one understands happiness. It is through pain, one has a sense of elation over joy. Therefore, just as one can change thought, one can change the way they feel through power of fixation within their mentality.

Power of fixation is in other words obsessive thinking or dominating thoughts. We often feel bad and do not want to feel this way, so much so that without even knowing subconsciously we become introspective. You are fighting with yourself and resisting these 'bad emotions' but by resisting you are becoming fixated with these feelings. My point is, do not pay attention to these upsetting emotions because 'emotion of attention' is a real thing. Remember, the philosophy of 'the law of expansion' on page 38 **_"What you focus on expands"_** and this applies to exactly with what is being mentioned here in regards to these emotions. When you feed attention to anything it expands, hence bad feelings beget bad feelings. As shortly stated by many 'nip it in the bud', meaning whenever you feel like that you need to 'eject' or press 'cancel' on these emotions before they overwhelm you.

Your feelings are an online basket and you choose what emotion you want to purchase through the currency of thought, anything you don't like 'press cancel'. You weaken your emotion by paying it little or no attention, therefore deliberately choose people, environments and thoughts that uplift your feelings or empower. Not those that leave you mentally drained and stultified as a result.

Thought is imagination, so why not imagine the best possible scenario until you feel it or it possibly happens. Adopt an optimistic attitude. You know often people say 'prepare for the worst and hope for the best', but lexically this means you are already at your worst so imagine the best outcome. You don't want to be in a position where you are thinking that thought of prepare for the worst. This to make one feel better through a simple change of thought and be pragmatic because sulking over a situation, 'throwing your toys out the pram' or being negative will not make your circumstance any better. For example, if you don't feel good today and you have a boxing match tomorrow, then not being mentally prepared could be a hiccup for disaster or loss. We are reactive to our feelings just as much as we are to our thoughts, both are equally responsive but it's what we choose to respond to. Therefore, think good, feel good and surely good will come your way. With hardship does come ease.

Today is tomorrow and yesterday was today, yesterday and tomorrow are all of the same thing in the sense that they offer a fresh opportunity to stimulate your thought and emotion. Many prudent people are consumed with what is to be, but it is how we live today that has an impact on what will be tomorrow. Today determines the future and the temporary present moment. In fact, I spent years in prison and I wanted to offer something back to the prison system to assist in rehabilitation. I manifested an idea named 'SIGNS Programme' in which I work with youth committing crime, and ex-offenders.

The slogan is "Changing Tomorrow, Today!"

One should understand completely that be pragmatic with being prudent. I do not suggest to abolish forward thinking for this is a sign of one's intelligence rather I encourage to debilitate negative thought for it can leave you short-sighted of life. There is no point in living in misery, worry or guilt. A wise Arab man once said:

"No amount of guilt can change the past and no amount of worrying can change the future".

There is endless thought to speculate at what could have been or what may happen but backward-thinking is like its name – a step backwards and life move on and so should you. Your life and character is determined by your train of thought and feeling. That is why I emphases and repeat so much about mindset continuously.

"Through your ability to think and feel, you have dominion over all creation" – Neville Goddard (1905-1972, New Thought Author)

Through your thought, you can create your own little world and live inside it without being disturbed. If you really really wanted to but it takes fortitude.

The way you think and feel may not necessarily effect anyone else's life, but it surely does make a difference to yours. Your thought and emotion serve as an invisible barrier that protects your well-being as you please.

Emotion is 'energy in motion'. The strength and vitality required to keep active is energy and motion is to put plans into action. Both are strongly relative to the contents within this chapter. Our energy levels and condition of energy whether it be positive or negative has a profound difference on our circumstances or environment as it takes shape due to our cognitive behaviour deriving from the root of our faculties (i.e. feeling and thought). Humans are sensitive creatures and we are prone to the sensation of feeling and thought, so use it to your advantage.

Mixed thoughts and feelings cause confusion leaving one unsure of life with no clarity, purpose, guidance or 'strong reason' to why one would want to achieve desired goals.

Bewilderment originates from fluctuation thoughts or emotions meaning sometimes we want this and sometimes we want that. Ultimately, leaving the human in a dormant state living a derelict life – if they do not detect or monitor their emotions. These feelings and emotions that shape our mindset timely, are just as effective as thought and when one controls their thinking process. Both split into two categories: positive and negative.

Most of the time negative thoughts pop up when one feels down and the way you think about matters effects the way you feel (vice versa), as a result effecting your behaviour plus attitude. Hence, it can be hard to grasp positive attitudes like gratitude. Remember on page 60, "Gratitude is attitude".

This matter of emotion can be confusing because you may presume you cannot change the way you feel or help the way you feel, but actually you can through a simple change of thought. Negative thoughts have a tendency to self-inject whether depressed or not and

111

you have to fend these off regularly. Negative thoughts are automated and are not always molded by logic or reason. These thoughts can be unrealistic or unreasonable serving no true purpose and are useless.

Such doom and gloom thoughts hold no value but you feed it attention constantly breeding value, meaning you make you believe something that is not necessarily true with weightless assumptions. In prison way too many times I would call a friend and they would not answer, suddenly I negatively suggest to myself that the worst or that I am a burden on them. The truth of the matter actually was that they was just busy at the time. Why think about what may or may not be true, it is like the who goes fishing where there may or may not be fish. What I mean is, there is no research to backup these negative thoughts. More than often it is just a myth you thought of in your head. You put yourself in a ambiguous scenario and do not truly know the reason or meaning behind what is happening or why.

Take matters easy with a stale perspective adopting patience, because the more you believe these self-damaging thoughts the more you tend to believe it and it exacerbates your feelings. The more you focus, the more it grows – you should scrunch up these thoughts and throw them away. Take some time out to compose yourself. Get your mental health state in a better place. Do not be melodramatic with your mind or exaggerate the negative. Jumping to conclusions is not healthy for the mind and

112

unnecessary time is wasted on useless worry. I will highlight five common traits of negative thinkers, so if you are aware and may avoid or counteract them.

1) Foolish Mindreading

We jump at unknown conclusions and assume, presume plus self-suggest matters that do not hold an iota of truth. For example, you may feel low as your mood shifts and assume others around you are behaving negatively towards you because you feel negative. We are not telepathic creatures, we do not know what others are thinking. Do not make up scenarios in your head. Do not wildly guess at that which may not even exist in the first place!

2) Diminution of Positive

This is when one ignores positive events and pays attention to negative things through their thoughts. For example, you may fall out with a friend and focus on the one negative argument rather than the years of good friendship you had! Do not make a micro issue into a macro problem is what I mean.

3) Exaggeration of Negative

Matters are bigger or worse than they seem. One may make something small into something big. For example, you may have had a relatively minor incident like accidently spilling juice on the sofa and become extremely worried that you spouse will react with upset. You become worried and end up lying which can cause trust issues. So you take an erratic or impulsive decision to buy new sofas as a present for your spouse. There are people like this in the world who over-exaggerate, do not be one of them. Most of the time your problems can be solved. I once read:

"Why worry over a problem that can be solved and if it cannot be solved, then why worry in the first place when there is no solution at all"

4) Over-defining
We give a scenario a bigger definition in our minds than what the matter actually appears on the surface. For example, you may not get along with a work colleague but you define this over the top by thinking nobody at work likes you!

5) Self-criticism (Misinterpretation)
This is when you take things personally that may not have even concerned you in the first place. For example, you may call a friend and they say 'they do not want to talk right now' but you take this personally thinking they do not want to talk to you. It could be they are busy or having a bad they themselves, and just wanted to take 'time out'.

Our thoughts are residents of our mind and sometimes we tend to pass chunks of time in our head ruminating, reflecting and focusing. This is fine, but the important part is the subject matter of what is being thought about. Pay attention to what matters.

You can change from negative to positive, but it is all in your mind! You can manage and reduce negativity. Here are five ways of doing so:

1) Binary Thinking
Filter your thoughts recognizing them to be either be one or the other (i.e. positive or negative). Awareness is the first step to transform your thinking process.

2) Value your thought
Realisation of what thought you have allows you to put a price tag on your thinking whether it is cheap (i.e. negative) or expensive (i.e. positive). What value do your thoughts truly have and this is determined by the reality of them because way too often negative thoughts are deemed to be not true and hold no value in reality whatsoever!

3) Choice of thought
If you could think of one thing to be true that you really wanted what would it be? This is known as envisaging, it shifts your thoughts away from negativity. I always do a thing called 'if you could take one thought to bed every night, what would it be?'. Make sure whatever it is, it is positive.

4) Release observation
Another word for observation is judgment. We are in a constant state of observing our surroundings and others, then casting judgment often negatively with bad things to think or say. By doing so allow something or someone else to live-rent free in your

head with your mental well-being at unrest.

5) Distract thoughts
Take your mind off things and be at ease with yourself. Reinforce a positive mind-set through engaging your thoughts – this is known as subconscious thinking. Distract your negative thinking by doing an activity you enjoy, otherwise known as therapeutic or creative activities.

Learn to tap into positivity by adopting dominating thoughts. Scrutinise your thinking (i.e. introspection). Positivity has a major impact on your life and makes your life more memorable. In the most sever circumstance as it is positivity that allows one to be optimistic. Ultimately, this improves your mental state as you feel you are happy and less down. Here are five tips for adopting positivity:

1) Practice gratitude
Be thankful for a lot even if you have been given little. Be grateful for your physical health (i.e. eyesight). Studies have shown that being grateful for even the smallest of things absolutely rids of negativity leaving one soaked in serenity making one feel uplifted, happy and even content. Make a list of things you are grateful for, start with your eyesight.

2) Self-scrutiny
Positivity is adopted through asking yourself questions, one being: 'Do I think positive?'. This allows you to tweak your thoughts in your favour to identify

116

your flaws and strengthen your mentality.

3) Association
Associate yourself with everything positive whether
it be words, people or your thoughts. Once you focus
on your inner self, then the outer self follows. Your
environment is a projection of your inner thoughts.
Develop your association with something as minor as
positive words is enough to indoctrinate the mind into
positivity. You are that which you associate with.

4) Analyse your strengths
Highlighting your strengths allows encouragement for
more room in improvement. Overlook the negative and
dwell on the positive through familiarizing yourself
with your thoughts. Think about something you've
achieved already or you like about yourself.

5) Power thinking
Power thinking is to think about thinking. Think why is
it the way you think, then think of ways to change the
way you think. They must be practical ways that are
lenient and you can achieve.

Keep in mind through introspection and self-
suggestion you can manipulate your circumstance
through attuning your disposition to positivity. This is
the way to gain 'emotional intelligence'.

I would advise going over this book again, highlighting
and making notes on anything applies to you.

PATIENCE AND GRATITUDE

Know that the most valuable facet within life is you!
In particular, your mind! What would life be without
you? Have you ever asked yourself that? Nothing!

If life had another name it would be problematic.
Every single human faces problems without doubt no
matter how affluent, famous or influential, yet none
of these factors make a difference on your state of
mind and how you perceive the world because it
something deeper within you that you give meaning to.

The same problem a rich man faces may be laughable
to a pauper and vice versa, but this is the epitome of
diversity in life all about shaping perception. Cling on
to positivity is the dominant message I have
portrayed constantly throughout the course of this
book. One of the strongest reason beings is because
positivity and adopting an optimistic attitude helped
me defeat strong thoughts of suicide. In fact, if it
wasn't for my optimism shaped by my religious views,
then I am sure this book would not be published
because I would have sadly committed suicide. This is
why you should take my words seriously within this
book. Two traits guaranteed to strengthen or adopt a
positive mind frame are patience and gratitude. It is
imperative for one to arm their self with these two
psychological guards when facing life itself.

Patience Is Ancient
Patience is old and old is gold as they say, and gold
holds great value. Patience strengthens the mind

118

resulting in fortitude. When physical strength is attained, the procedure is for the body to follow a regime of physical exercise straining the body in order to strengthen it and the same applies for when strengthening the mind, whereby one will inevitably undergo hardship in life – this being a prerequisite for patience. How can one be patient, if there is nothing to be patient about?

The truth is there is no gift better than patience. This ancient ethos of patience allows you to build a thick skin metaphorically making your character impenetrable. As you stroll down this street named life, you must investigate yourself – who you are and where you are going. Unequivocally, you will face tests that are unpredictably thrown in your path but being armed with patience allows you to dodge or overcome these hurdles of issues. This quality of patience to your character is like carbon to steel!

When patience is truly exercised, one feels serenity. There is a dire need for this golden trait for every generation because a life without patience can be unbearable. Anyone who has experienced the blissful effects of patience will admit that the best days are those that were molded around patience.

"Life consists of two days. One day for you and one day against. The day it is for you display gratitude and the day it is against you display patience"
– Ali ibn Talib

The citation is from a Muslim leader in the 6th century who was famously known worldwide at this time for his leadership and sound judgment. Outlandishly, patience in Arabic is pronounced as 'sabr' and it is to refrain, resist, detain or stop. In essence, patience means to prevent one's self from panic and despair, moaning, complaining or exaggerating grief.

Patience is a dose of medicine for the mind and viewed as a positive psychological attitude. Humans rush to that which benefits us, yet when it comes to patience we seem to be turning away strangely. To live a regulated life with a healthy mindset can hardly be grasped without some form of patience. Ideally, one who is patient is one who is well-trained in handling difficulties through self-control, as they calmly accept life's trials. Patience is a sign of maturity and intelligence, generally it is to shut your mouth, work hard, be ambitious and get on with life.

Panic is a problem and you cannot solve a problem with a problem, therefore solution being patience. Some people exercise such great patience that you would not be able to tell the difference if they were in hardship or ease. Once I moaned about a friend's death of mine to my next door neighbor in prison whom returned a stale look replying: "my mum died this week, but you have to be patient". Overall, we feel difference between struggle and ease, but it is the odd few who can remain the same in ease and hard times through their levels of patience.

We are incentive creatures and always working towards something, so to have patience also means that your motive and common sense outwits any lust or desire. As humans we have a lustful capacity, but this is tamed through patience (i.e. common sense and motive). For example, a boxer may enjoy sexual intercourse but debauchery leads to detrimental health, therefore his common sense knows this and suggests to act differently towards another motive. One of that which will benefit his vocation and health through remaining patience and having gratitude, this also allows discipline to blossom in his life.

There is such a thing as weak or strong patience. Some may have patience when it comes to one matter, yet completely become impatient with another situation. This is known as weak patience, whereas someone else has the ability to hug patience no matter what the circumstance with unwavering courage allowing them to bear any calamity.

We are always in a state of 'staying away' or 'drawing towards', otherwise known as 'driving' or 'restraining'. You are either drawing towards benefits or staying away from harm whether that is physically, mentally or even one's surroundings such as: company and environment. Patience is required in both of these fields; those who can exercise patience in both scenarios are strong contenders of being a prime example of one who has a strong level of patience. The definition of patience it itself is to have the ability to accept delay or trouble calmly, yet in different scenarios different types of patience may be exerted. You may not have this characteristic in an innate manner, but you can develop it through practice and it allows you to adopt it making you accustomed to patience regularly.

Everyone has had to be patient at some moment in their life either with or without choice. There are four types of common patience:
1) Psychological patience by choice
2) Psychological patience without choice
3) Physical patience with choice
4) Physical patience without choice

The first is to stay away from things, which your common sense advises are wrong.

The second is the name patience itself; you really do not an option but to resort to patient eventually, just like when you lose someone that you love.

The third is when one exerts effort; be it labour commonly whereby patience is appropriate.

The fourth is when you experience severe weather or illness for this is beyond human scope or choice.

Patience can be summarised as a mental battle between reason (intellect) versus lust (desire). If a person's patience is strong they will not succumb to their whims. Some philosophers and scholars agree that: "if a person's lust overcomes their intellect, then they are animalistic". This is because animals do not have the extent of faculty of reason like us humans and they indulge in desires like debauchery. Overall, when desire prevails often intellect becomes debilitated. On the flip side of things, when intellect avails often lust becomes weakened. This is because one weighs up the benefits and harm chasing the appropriate course of action.

Psychological battle is another name for patience. A constant war between motives of reason and the forces of lust. Both fluctuate providing what inmate faculty is stronger at the time or onset of a moment. Where one strengthens, the other weakens. Inevitably, we all face difficulty; therefore anticipating patience is almost a must.

Bad patience is impatience or when one willingly remains reclusive from their set goals. A purpose-driven life is helpful to mental well-being and there is tons of evidence supporting this as psychologists have proven. Patience is needed in help, aid or seeking anything favourable in your life.

Important to note is that we have the tendency to complain, moan or grief but that is normal and this does not contradict our level of patience. Show me a human who does not feel when their condition changes, but it is how we react to these scenarios.

The impatient one can be referred to as 'the ignorant' and the patient one can be referred to as 'the noble, because the noble person exerts patience willingly, where as 'the ignorant' knows of patience with all its benefits, yet walks on the path of being impatient regardless. This silly decision is a reflection of one's character, reason and intellect, because although they choose to be impatient in a rush; eventually every single person will have to adopt patience sooner or later. Patience is like the weather it is unavoidable and so just like the weather (i.e. a storm) that causes difficulty sometimes – we must wrap ourselves up with heart-warming patience.

A wise man once said:
"a noble one as soon as calamity appears does that which an ignorant one does after a month"

Meaning, the noble one turns to patience immediately being pragmatic, whereas the ignorant one turns tot patience when their impatience runs out and has no other choice but to finally turn towards patience in the end unwillingly when they should have done so in the first place for their own benefit.

Being noble saves your dignity, so instead of turning to everyone else for help sometimes you can just save yourself from simply displaying patience and give it time. Things will get better and you will find a solution. Time is a healer as they say.

Don't you know the impatient one achieves almost

nothing, whereas the patient one achieves part of his aims. In life there are matters beyond our control, the sooner you realise this truth the better. Being impatient is useless, so patience as it allows a reasonable psychological reaction. Where one would usually respond with panic, grief, despair and discontentment – it is eradicated if not faded through patience breeding the opposite – contentment, serenity, gratitude and acceptance.

The only way to strengthen patience is to practice it, as this allows you to fortify this golden quality. Patience is medicinal as it cures grief, sorrow, distress and more. It is a 'psychological pill' that allows one to think of consequence, bear it in mind and relish the idea or solution that is most sensible to one's state of mind. We live in a world of cause and effect; therefore it is sound reason that triggers patience. It is reason that allows contemplation and directs our thoughts to that which is most beneficial for anyone (i.e. patience).

Patience is a must! We cannot do without it and it is a necessity. Ease does not last forever, this life is temporary regardless of health, wealth, enjoyment, security – all these physical gratifications have an expiry date unknown to you and I. a wise person does exult in pride in times of ease or show extreme despair in time of hardship, therefore be moderate adopting humbleness through patience in both good and bad times in life.

To gain even a fraction of patience is mentally straining and requires one to be constantly introspective, but due to our natural aversion or inherent laziness towards and task we become 'stupid' or lack intelligence as we fail to exercise the most important muscle, which is our brain and the faculty of thinking.

Thoughts are a condiment for the mind making life palatable, but even behind transforming your thoughts or training your thinking to be positive requires patience. Only the foolish and ignorant abandon the quest of knowledge in pursuit of pleasure and hedonism. You can never be a 'know-it-all' or be content with the amount of knowledge you possess because it is never-ending when you're a student of life. You be a 'learn-it-all' as we are always in a state of learning but it requires zeal and it was only through being struck with the misfortune of being confined to a prison cell for nearly a decade due to my young silly mistakes that I had enough of being stupid, so I decide to study and read and write.

I kept making stupid decisions leading to stupid scenarios resulting in me sitting stupidly in prison, but I vowed to myself I would not make any more stupid suggestions to myself and use my time wisely as a blessing, which many fail to realise.

Muhammed (peace be upon him) said: "Two blessings that people are unaware of are health and free time"

These two things I had in abundance in prison and I utilised to its utmost, but nevertheless along with patience at the forefront allowed me to sharpen my mentality and develop my thinking process.

Thinking stops you from being absent-minded and so take time out for yourself to reflect on your mind, circumstance plus what you can offer to the world and others because not everything in life is about you – learn to be lenient, compassionate and emphatic.

Patience is easy for those who make it easy and it is difficult for those who make it difficult for their own self. The strength of our patience is determined by one's motive. For example, a rich man may find it hard to abstain from chasing physical gratifications with all that wealth as a means at his dispense, whereas a pauper can exercise patience with ease as he is not tested with the trial of wealth. Another parable may be that since testerone levels rise in youth and are often high, a young may struggle finding it difficult to abstain from fornication, whereas the elderly person has no such issue remaining patient with ease. My point is:

"Our level of patience is determined largely upon our circumstance, but more importantly our disposition"

This is because when you have 'the means' to do or follow such actions, remaining patience can make it harder or difficult. For example, god knows we are incentive creatures so whoever follows the holy commands and abstains from sins will be rewarded with paradise in the hereafter, therefore one uses reason and intellect to weigh up the options of 'motive versus lust' resulting in a decision that should be sound, as they have weak patience they may err, whereas the one with strong patience has the power of abstinence plus self-control.

I have spoken to many women plus men who admit the regret that follows in their pursuit of happiness or pleasure. They sought sexual intercourse hoping for an ephemeral satisfaction but were left with long-lasting regret and in the end confess the best option was to refrain through remaining patience in the first place. Patience is more bearable than the pain of remorse, so when one realises this truth they should choose the lighter option but such is the pursuit of pleasure it is a big deception.

Truth be told we are always in need of patience as we are constantly in the state of 'action or abstinence' whether you realise it or not. We are either drawing closer to something or staying away from something and in both matters patience is required. The ability to have a plan or desired, carry out the appropriate action whilst remaining patience from anything harmful that opposes to your plans, still requires a level of patience at the end of the day.

It is down to you how to respond or answer to your minds thoughts because life is filled with temptations, distractions but you need to call upon your focus and attention to help you live a better life for your own mental well-being. You can adopt this through positive forces like patience and gratitude because patience is ancient and gratitude is attitude.

Gratitude is Attitude

Gratitude can be described shortly in two words 'recognise blessings'. Gratitude is to be grateful, thankful and appreciative. Patience and gratitude are two sides of the same coin. The equipment of the patient and the investment of the grateful promote a positive attitude. Patience is the mother and Gratitude is the father which pregnates positivity.

Both patience and gratitude are a state of mind, which can be cultivated through acknowledgment plus use. It allows you to have a new parameter of judgment, remove and install a new mentality. You have to implement both patience and gratitude to maximize its fruits as portal application results in imbalance. Hence, people are patient because they have no choice, yet are not thankful.

Nourishing is patience and gratitude for the mind, in the same way that food and drink nourish the body or faith and prayer nourish the soul. The spectrum of these two qualities differ from person to person solely upon the mind and its train of thought. Polish the condition of your mind through pragmatic thinking, which should lead you to adopting patience and gratitude. Thoughts will enter your awareness and your attention will follow them, no matter how many times this happen just keep ringing your focus back to your priorities and what really matters as this allows you to move forward.

Invest in your mind, meaning train your thought process to powerful thinking. Thinking about your thoughts recognizing which ones are negative in order to eradicate them is like metaphorically your brain being a hard drive and you unscrew it, take it out and polish it, so it can work smoother when installed back in to the network of your mind. It is similar to when you reboot a computer so it comes back refreshed, ready for you to use and progress. Thinking truly is a condiment for the mind allowing you to sprinkle positive qualities such as: patience and gratitude.

The only person you need to prove a point to is yourself. There is no point getting your point across to pointless people. You decide who is pointless in your life. Think about that and expand your thinking, for life manifests from thoughts. Train your thoughts just like you would your body. Use the heavy valued weight of patience and gratitude.

Your mind is like a deposit bank, so only allow 'thoughts of value' to be deposited, positive thoughts are the most expensive currency to be accepted only!

Analyse your mind (i.e. thoughts) what behaviours or emotions do you need control or tackle. Are you grateful or do you lack gratitude, are you patient or impatient? Introspection, self-scrutiny, self-analysis are all signs of an intelligent person forming rectitude eventually paving a way to one's achievement or goals. Recognising your state of mind could be one of your greatest acknowledgements in life. Your state of mind could be one of your greatest acknowledgments in life. Your inner (i.e. subconscious thought) is a wonderful place and powerful tool unscrewing tightly fixed negative thoughts to be released. You can cure a mental illness such as: depression, sorrow, grief or anxiety through a simple change of thought by adopting a new mentality.

I never 'thought' I'd be an author infusing my experience and pain to share with so many people especially at the onset of my prison sentence when I was severely depressed negotiation with myself to end my life in a prison cell or not, but through 'positive 'thought' the outcome was different.

Sometimes you never know the value of a moment until it becomes a memory, in the same way you will never be able to empower your mind until you go through hardship, as this is a perquisite for fortitude. You have to go through something negative to turn it into a positive and that is the best way I can describe this book.

Through this mental transition fortitude is built as a tower of strength to the mind. Patience nor gratitude cannot be replaced by any other mental jewel for it is irreplaceable. A life without either of these qualities becomes like an emotional ticking time bomb ready to explode causing self-destruction through negative emotion spilling out like those mentioned on page 24.

The past is a recess of the mind. Do not let your past allow you to lose hope of the future. Any coveted aim in life hugely dependent upon patience and gratitude.

*"Those who are not thankful for a little,
how will they then be thankful for a lot?"*

Practice being grateful for the smaller things in life. Make it a habit. How you do anything is how you do everything. You have to begin from somewhere.

In a prison cell often I would get lost swimming in a sea of thoughts that would serve to be positive my mental well-being. Experience allows foresight; you cannot gain hindsight without going through an experience itself. This is why many people often say 'What I went through made me who I am" because they made a transition not allowing their past to determine their future outcome in life.

Life can be what the mind perceives. It is the process of affirmation and visualisation. A life filled with blessings that sometimes we often fail to see. Even the smallest things like appreciating eyesight. Even myself sometimes do err and forget. Underestimating health not realizing how truly privileged we are to even walk, just ask the disabled who cannot walk; the mute or deaf about their health!

Some people contain ingratitude, at the expense of gratitude. Ingratitude is the main ingredient as a recipe for 'unsettled thoughts' as a sour dish being served to the mind. Ingratitude can cause lead you to being envious.

Envy is mental astigmatism and a 'psychological disease'. Always discontented writing for what others have is like trying to obtain blood from a stone and we know this is not possible. No matter how much you envy it will not change your circumstance. Only working hard, being motivated, making calculated decisions and displaying patience with gratitude truly will change things for you in your life.

You cannot melt yourself into someone else's personality, so arm yourself with patience and wrestle hardship to the ground. Patience is not to sulk or complain but always seek the good things in life. This is how you identify gratitude and make the best out of a worst situation. Do not envy others, we all suffer in silence. Everyone faces challenges.

Behind every pain, challenge or struggle in life is unknown wisdom foreign to every human that we may never comprehend. I am a strong believer of 'everything happens for a reason', but we may not necessarily always know that reason and sometimes never ever find out. You have to accept things for what they are in life especially if it is beyond our control. All we truly have is patience and gratitude.

133

CONCLUSION

Do not grief over what is to be or what is to come, had we even the opportunity to be one of the world's most influential people – you could still not influence the unprecedented and unpredictable future. Look at the worlds presidents and kings, no matter how much they try to govern a country or prepare for the worst, they cannot.

A modern day prime example is covid-19, which struck the world effecting everyone., take matters easy and do not be hard on yourself even through life itself may be hard. We cannot save the world but we can remain patient and be good or kind to everyone that we cross paths with in this journey named life.

Accept there will never be an egalitarian society in any corner of this unsettled world no matter what democracy appears, any politician says or any constituency being represented. A democratic world is a life of division due to opposing parties with no liberal approach.

Humans are intricate creatures forever prone to being quarrelsome; therefore politics, society even religion causes division and animosity. The world we live in today is diverse, hence filled with turmoil there is no truly followed principles set for equality in society.

As Bob Marley stated in a famous song: *'so much trouble in the world'*, yet this trouble is caused by the inhabitants of the earth – us humans. We cannot change the world but we can change ourselves. There is a real need for constant rectification, growth and self-development whether that be set through guidelines of religion, or even self-counsel, but one thing I can say confidently is patience can and only will benefit you, it can do no harm.

Man knows what's best for man. Woman knows what's best for woman. We know what's best for our self. There will always be a colossal divide amongst countries and humans but you must unite with your inner self drawing closer to a life of serenity.

Sometimes even I question myself, when alone sat in a dark prison cell realizing the dark world we live in, filled with my deep thoughts; that you know surely there must be more to life than this life, which is so mundane filled with jobs of drudgery. The monotony of having a repetitive routine for ten, twenty or thirty years straight.

There has been too many injustices gone unscathed for our souls to just remain in this transient earth. It cannot be that the end of the world manifests from the destruction of our own hands as climate debilitates and elements of this world exacerbate or just wait for an apocalypse. Surely, there is more to this life than this life. There has to be a hereafter.

Reading is all I done in prison and I became a recluse as my books became my companions. It allowed me to broaden the horizon of my mind brightening my face instead of being a sad criminal, yet this was only possible for me through patience and I do not know anything else like it but its name (i.e. patience).

Life is too short just ask the one in the grave. I have an older brother who died when I was aged eight. Now, I am twenty-eight. Twenty years just went like twenty seconds for me. God knows where or what I will be doing in twenty years from now.

I am a Muslim and the religion I believe in is Islam which is strongly shaped around this golden ethos of patience, but ultimately in a troubled world it allows me to be calm giving me the opportunity to live a life of tranquility with a health body, free mind and peaceful soul away from all the troubles of this world knowing there is a hereafter, for which everything in this world will be accounted for with our actions and this belief really gives me a sense of peace daily.

Studying and education is the biggest tool in life. Learn to be autodidact. Educate yourself. There is nothing in comparison to the scopes of education. Learning and sharing knowledge. I do not know of anything greater than that in my years of being alive.

Life is often not about a change in circumstance,
but a change in perspective.
What I mean by this is, so many people yearn to be
'rich' and have money with the belief life will be much
smoother if their circumstances changed, which does
hold a bit of truth but this can only happen if you
have a change in perspective towards the world. I had
the same mentality but it has changed slightly as I
have added philanthropy into this perspective of
mine, which completely changed my life. Helping
others gives me more of a satisfaction than getting
money itself, it is far more rewarding.

 It is about shifting how we view the world and
perceive relationships because humans live according
to their view, yet by changing this response we can
transform our lives dramatically. Train your personal
thought process to suit any life orientation you
choose.

All I can say is I studied and read a hell of a lot in
prison to really try to figure out life plus what do I
want. I came to the conclusion of being a
philanthropist. To help those in need and share
knowledge. Hence, I publish books and have projects
I am still working on till today like my knife crime
charity, youth programme and doing motivational talks
at schools to inspire the younger generation to teach
them knowledge I wish I had at their age to help
them flourish in life.

Printed in Great Britain
by Amazon

87012597R00078